# BEYOND THE SCHOOL:

## Community and Institutional Partnerships in Art Education

edited by

Rita L. Irwin
*University of British Columbia*

*and*

Anna M. Kindler
*University of British Columbia*

D0818550

1999

The National Art Education Association

## About NAEA

Founded in 1947, the National Art Education Association is the largest professional art education association in the world. Membership includes elementary and secondary teachers, artists, administrators, museum educators, arts council staff, and university professors from throughout the United States and abroad. NAEA's mission is to advance art education through professional development, service, advancement of knowledge, and leadership.

**Cover:** Minneapolis, Minnesota. Peavey Park is situated in the Phillips neighborhood of Minneapolis. The Phillips Gateway Project, originally commissioned by the Minneapolis Arts Commission and funded with both public and private dollars, is an important part of the effort to build community and create neighborhood identity in this part of the city. Rafala Green, project artist/coordinator, presented a proposal that would not only create a public artwork on a site of community significance, but would create wide ranging opportunities to involve the community in its making. Since 1992, in addition to projects in schools, community art workshops were established to offer mentoring and training for the young people of Phillips. Professional artists worked directly with teenagers from the area developing designs for benches and walkways that extended to the actual making and installation of the rich tile and mosaic structures. It has been a massive and ongoing undertaking that has involved more than 1,000 young people in educational opportunities and provided employment for a large number of teenagers and adults.

ISBN 1-890160-09-1

# TABLE OF CONTENTS

Art Education Beyond School Boundaries:  Identifying Resources, Exploring Possibilities
*Anna M. Kindler and Rita L. Irwin* . . . . . . . . . . . . . . . . . . . . . . . . . . . . . . . . . . . . . . . . 1

## Part I
## Communities as a Place to Begin

Where Community Happens
  *Robin E. Clark* . . . . . . . . . . . . . . . . . . . . . . . . . . . . . . . . . . . . . . . . . . . . . . 5
Hawaii:  Arts Education Partnerships in a Diverse Community
  *Peggy Hunt* . . . . . . . . . . . . . . . . . . . . . . . . . . . . . . . . . . . . . . . . . . . . . . . . . 14
Commonwealth Games, Showcase for Visual Art
  *Robert Dalton* . . . . . . . . . . . . . . . . . . . . . . . . . . . . . . . . . . . . . . . . . . . . . . 21
School-Community Collaboration and Artistic Process
  *Jacques-Albert Wallot and Bruno Joyal* . . . . . . . . . . . . . . . . . . . . . . . . . . . . . . 29
Art Education Wrapped/Trapped in Fun:  The Hope and Flight of Recreation
Centre Art Instructors
  *Lara M. Lackey* . . . . . . . . . . . . . . . . . . . . . . . . . . . . . . . . . . . . . . . . . . . . . 36

## Part II
## Voices Within Communities

Moving the Mountain:  Linking Higher Art Education and Communities
  *Fiona Dean* . . . . . . . . . . . . . . . . . . . . . . . . . . . . . . . . . . . . . . . . . . . . . . . . *47*
The Dinner Party
  *Philip J. Perry* . . . . . . . . . . . . . . . . . . . . . . . . . . . . . . . . . . . . . . . . . . . . . 57
Art as a Way of Learning:  A Business and Education Partnership
  *Patricia Pinciotti and Rebecca Gorton* . . . . . . . . . . . . . . . . . . . . . . . . . . . . . . 63
Literacy and Visual Culture in Three Art Gallery Settings
  *Lon Dubinsky* . . . . . . . . . . . . . . . . . . . . . . . . . . . . . . . . . . . . . . . . . . . . . 70
The Artemisia Project:  School, Artists, University and Museum Partnership
  *Ann Calvert* . . . . . . . . . . . . . . . . . . . . . . . . . . . . . . . . . . . . . . . . . . . . . . 80
Matrix, Meaning and Metacognition
  *Cheryl Meszaros* . . . . . . . . . . . . . . . . . . . . . . . . . . . . . . . . . . . . . . . . . . . 88

Contributors . . . . . . . . . . . . . . . . . . . . . . . . . . . . . . . . . . . . . . . . . . . . . . 95

# INTRODUCTION

## Art Education Beyond School Boundaries:
## Identifying Resources, Exploring Possibilities

Anna M. Kindler and Rita L. Irwin
*University of British Columbia*

In recent years, much attention has been drawn in education to learning that occurs beyond school boundaries. Understanding education in contexts broader than schooling has important implications for art education and calls for an examination of alternative venues, initiatives and strategies that facilitate artistic development, encourage aesthetic growth and promote reflection about the role and value of art in a society. While learning sites such as museums have received some attention in recent art education literature (e.g, Irwin & Rogers, 1998; Kindler, 1998; Storr, 1998; Vallance, 1995), the contribution of communities and institutions, not specifically designated as agents of culture, towards art education has been only marginally explored. Yet, as this anthology demonstrates, these communities and institutions constitute rich and valuable resources and contexts in which learning in art, through art, and about art can effectively take place.

This collection of essays was put together to present a strong rationale for collaborative partnerships that extend education in the arts beyond the school boundaries by demonstrating benefits that stem from such collaborative initiatives. This anthology was also envisioned to present a range of possibilities in developing art education alliances that bring together various constituencies and give due recognition to community-based education. Our ambition was not to undermine the value and importance of formal, systematic art education in school settings, but rather to explore ways in which learning that begins at school can be extended and supported by resources that reside within the broader community, highlighting ways in which learning can be enriched through the participation and involvement of new, outside partners able to contribute expertise, insight, and funds not readily available in schools. We were also committed to bringing attention to the need for extending education in the arts beyond school-aged populations by simultaneously

encouraging and implementing new ways of engaging adolescents and adults outside the school system to become lifelong learners in the arts.

This anthology begins with a consideration of the concept of community
through an examination of the nature of social relations that support and encourage a climate conducive to nurturing and valuing of the arts. Robin Clark contrasts
the notions of collectivity and community and argues that a genuine community is
not based on consensus or conformity to the conditions defined by its most vocal
constituents, but rather builds on respect and recognition of multiple voices and
perspectives. It is this context of true openness to diversity that provides a platform
for art education initiatives that are broad, bold and relevant to a community at
large. The concept of a "genuine community" to which Clark refers is further
explored in the two parts of this anthology.

The first block of chapters focuses on identification and exploration of places for
the arts within a community and offers a discussion of selected aspects of community cultures that support a fertile ground for artistic and aesthetic learning. Peggy
Hunt describes the field of art education in Hawaii, framing it within the notion of
a community that draws on the tremendously rich cultural resources of the island.
Hunt describes how bridging local and immigrant cultures has come together to
create a multifaceted, multiracial, and multicultural society where many aspects of
life are imbued with art and artmaking.

Ways in which arts can become integrated with other aspects of life in a society
are explored by Robert Dalton who describes the recent Commonwealth Games as
a showcase for visual arts. The world of sports, which has a strong appeal in many
Western societies, is seen by Dalton as a space open for arts' involvement and education that grow from common interests. He highlights the role of the arts in the
organization of the games from architectural design of competition venues,
through choreography, stage and costume design for the opening ceremonies,
games logos and advertising, to many exhibitions of artwork and art demonstrations that accompanied the event. Dalton is careful to recognize both the opportunity that large sport festivals provide for arts advocacy, promotion and education,
as well as the contribution that arts make to the success of such events.

The significance, importance, and value of art education sites outside of school
boundaries are emphasized by Lara Lackey. Referring to art education in community centers as an education both "wrapped and trapped in fun," Lackey offers an
insightful analysis that contrasts stereotypical ways of thinking about art in a community center with the reality and potential of artistic learning in these contexts.
Lackey's essay is grounded in a research project which involved interviews and
ethnographic observations of community center-based art educators and provides a
well formulated argument for more serious consideration of community centers as
agents for arts advocacy and arts learning.

In the closing chapter of the first section of this anthology Jacques-Albert Wallot
and Bruno Joyal offer their reflection on the school unit as a community. They

argue that a school culture provides an excellent platform for collective work and elaborate on the nature of a learning process in art which relies on group work and collaboration. Wallot and Joyal present a case for art activities where iconographic changes occur and aesthetic choices are broadened through implementation of collective strategies drawn from the world of art and supported by sensitive pedagogy.

What models could be proposed to those interested in implementing collaborative initiatives in art education? The second part of this anthology offers some answers to this question. Fiona Dean describes a number of community-based urban projects designed to beautify neighborhoods, parks, and housing projects through collaborative networks of institutions and community groups. Her rich project descriptions from diverse regions of the world celebrate partnerships focused on resolving challenging issues. These collaborations have not only promoted and provided learning opportunities in the arts, but have also explored the role of the arts as an agent of social change and justice. Dean is committed to the idea that in order to be relevant and address the real needs of a society, institutions of higher learning need to be more outgoing and innovative in the ways in which they recruit and engage their students and faculty, and explore forms of partnerships outside of the traditional boundaries of academia.

The mandate for universities to reach out is further advocated by Phil Perry whose chapter reflecting upon "The Dinner Party" initiative offers a good example of successful institutional links between various art education stakeholders. Perry describes how Monash University in Victoria, Australia, a local arts center and art gallery, along with 15 elementary schools, came together in sponsoring an art event that touched the entire community and generated much interest and enthusiasm for the arts. This example demonstrates how benefits of collaborative partnerships can extend well beyond those initially involved and can enrich the cultural environment of an entire community.

In times where funding for art education in schools suffers and teachers face the challenge to deliver quality art education with shrinking resources, it is essential to explore possibilities of partnerships that would help fund this important area of the curriculum. While such explorations need to proceed with caution to ensure the integrity of the educational process, there are numerous possibilities of worthwhile art education initiatives situated within the realm of corporate interests. A cooperative project between the Northampton Community College and the Binney & Smith, Inc. described in Pat Pinciotti and Rebecca Gorton's chapter offers an example of how educational and business interests can be negotiated and how sensitive corporate sponsorship can benefit education in the arts.

The last three chapters of this anthology focus on collaborative endeavors involving museums. Lon Dubinsky reports on the "Reading the Museum" project where education in the arts and the development of literacy skills go hand in hand. Dubinsky's analysis of this undertaking emphasizes the challenge that museums face in reaching a diverse public. He advocates for a greater recognition of the museum as "a narrative place" and for development of community-based partner-ships that take advantage of this space in serving needs and interests of all partici-pants. The Artemisia Project, which is the focus of Ann Calvert's chapter, was initi-ated to test the effectiveness of an art curriculum for gender equity and involved a partnership of high school students and their teachers, eight women artists, a muse-um curator, and university faculty. This successful initiative explored a mentorship model and allowed students to study the work of local artists, document artistic careers, and contribute to the development of permanent curriculum resources. It also involved an interactive exhibition of both the accomplished and beginning artists. Once again, the impact of this project on the community and the impor-tance of learning situated within and drawing on community resources are high-lighted in Calvert's contribution.

Cheryl Meszaros has the final word in this discussion centered around new pos-sibilities of delivering art education and the role institutions and agencies other than schools can play in furthering this cause. Backed with experience as a director of educational programs at a major urban art gallery, Meszaros eloquently argues for transformation of museums into learning places that are dynamic, interactive, and responsive to the diverse needs of diverse audiences. She provides an account of specific initiatives that were devised at the Vancouver Art Gallery to further this goal and offers a wealth of advice on how museums can complement art education in the schools and effectively cater to the needs of visitors of all ages.

The themes of collaboration, partnership, and community are central to this anthology and the articles compiled in this volume speak about the potential, bene-fits, as well as challenges that they involve. They offer encouragement and words of wisdom born out of experience and careful reflection to guide development of new alliances drawing on and strengthening communities through an arts involvement. We hope that the reflections and examples this anthology provides will lead to a proliferation of successful initiatives where schools, universities, museums, commu-nity-based institutions, as well as businesses and corporations will come together to fulfill their social responsibility by promoting lifelong learning while encouraging education through art and in art.

## References

Irwin, R. L., & Rogers, T. (1998). Inspirations for four circles/soaring visions. In Tandanya National Aboriginal Cultural Institute (Eds.), *Four circles/soaring visions* (pp. 1-2). Adelaide, South Australia: Author.

Kindler, A. M. (1998). Aesthetic development and learning in art museums: A challenge to enjoy. *Journal of Museum Education, 22*(2 & 3), 12-16.

Storr, A. V. F. (1998). On learning studies, policy, philosophy, and what we know about essential expe-riences of art in museums. *Journal of Museum Education, 22*(2 & 3), Part 1, 17-19.

Vallance, E. (1995). The public curriculum of orderly images. *Educational Researcher, 24*(2), 4-13.

Part I

# Communities as a Place to Begin

## Where Community Happens

Robin E. Clark

*Minot State University*

Whatever their motives, when the stark isolation of individualism becomes hollow and intolerable, human beings generally turn toward others with whom they perceive some basis for establishing relation (Dowrick, 1991). We in the field of art education are no exception. In our attempts to establish and maintain an increasingly vital professional community, it becomes necessary to reflect on and analyze possible forms of societal relationships in order to suggest conditions necessary for genuine collaboration.

To provide a means for our "self-examination," philosophical tenets of Buber (1958; 1965) are used to present two opposing organizational models: "community" and "collectivity." Next, three social/educational issues currently enjoying a relatively high degree of exposure and active contemplation among art educators are identified and briefly examined within Buber's models of "community" and "collectivity." Finally, several potential implications for the art education professional community are discussed.

## Collectivity And The Individual

Although the word "collective" is commonly used in the English language as a synonym for "community," Buber (1965) makes definite distinctions between the two. In Buber's terminology, a *collectivity* or *collective* is made up of those who have, in effect, surrendered self in order to become an accepted part of a larger group. *Individualism*, whether by choice or default, may be described as the isolated and/or insulated existence and efforts of a solitary being. In a collective, individuals are "packed together, armed and equipped in common..." (Buber, 1965, p. 31).

Buber (1965) suggests that the young, in particular, have tended to blindly devote themselves to collectives through a "fear of being left, in this age of confusion, to rely on themselves..." and an "unconscious desire to have responsibility removed from them by an authority in which they believe or want to believe" (p. 115). Although the "age of confusion" mentioned by Buber actually took place some 50-plus years ago, our world today is no less chaotic for young and old alike. Paradigm shifts abound, values collide, traditions wax and wane (Freedman, 1994a), all accompanied by a growing measure of uncertainty regarding the future.

As a direct result of such an atmosphere, many isolated individuals turn to the security of organizations upon which they feel they can rely for direction and guidance. One expectation is that the combined wisdom of the group and the visions of its leaders will somehow determine and articulate for members an appropriate set of questions and answers to the most confusing and troublesome issues of the day. However, in their attempts to find direction and purpose, those who join organizations often surrender (by default) their personal responsibility for making critical decisions. In the process, they may allow themselves to be caught up and carried along by trendy sorts of movements and causes being championed and promoted by the organization of which they are members. Unfortunately, when this happens often enough on an individual basis, the "whole" gradually deteriorates into a mere collective of weak, ineffective, solitary beings, rather than developing into an active, vitally functioning community. May (1994) speaks for many when she says: "...I try not to think much about these structural constraints and organizational arrangements, those ties that bind us in oppressive, depressing ways. Such conditions make me feel...sad, impotent, and fraudulent..." (p. 140).

The irony is that for the individual who was originally seeking to conquer his or her isolation by joining a group, a collective rarely holds any answers. On the contrary, according to Buber (1965), the isolation of individualism has not been dispelled, but merely "overpowered and numbed" (p. 201). That is, the individual is not able to break out of isolation through membership in the collective, rather, he or she has simply traded one brand of isolation for another, that of being lost in the crowd. This occurs because "collectivity is based on an organized atrophy of personal existence..." (p. 31).

Having sought to leave behind the oppressive isolation of individualism and find some sense of community within the ranks of an organization, the hapless individual may discover instead an increased loss of personal identity, voice, efficacy, and responsibility within the dense confines of a collective. In cases such as this, "the collectivity becomes what really exists, the person becomes derivatory" (Buber, 1965, p. 80).

## The Genuine Third Alternative

Fortunately, there is a third alternative to suffering as an individual or to being absorbed by the collective, and that is the participation in a "genuine community." Buber (1965) says, "...by 'genuine' being understood a point of view which cannot be reduced to one of the first two [i.e., individualism or collectivity], and does not represent a mere compromise between them" (p. 202). In other words, a genuine community is something more than the best that either (or a combination of) individualism or collectivism is able to offer. Membership in a collective is tantamount to a surrender of self, while membership in a genuine community requires "a pledge of self" (p. 32). The individual who pledges self to a community, pledges personal responsibility for decisive action and meaningful involvement, not passive and tacit support. In fact, as May (1994) claims: "A community both requires us and frees us to speak and to act in more reasonable, compassionate ways..." (p. 138).

This "genuine third alternative" of community begins very simply in a special place Buber calls "the between" (1958; 1965, p. 202). In the "between," individuals and groups are able to meet and commune openly and freely with others in dialogic relation. Neither is objectified by the other, they meet in equality as subject with subject. Buber (1965) claims,

> ...community, growing community...is the being no longer side by side but *with* one another of a multitude of persons. And this multitude, though it also moves toward one goal, yet experiences everywhere a turning to, a dynamic facing of, the other, a flowing from *I* to *Thou* [original italics]. (p. 31)

The dialogue that ensues occurs in the neutral zone "between" the two participants, not from some lopsided vantage point which favors one over the other (Clark-Winright, 1991). There is no contest or competition involved, no seeking to bend or subvert the will of the other, no self-serving attitudes or postures. There is present a sense of genuine respect, trust, collegiality, mutuality of purpose, and wholehearted acceptance of differences. "There are no gifted and ungifted here, only those who give themselves and those who withhold themselves" (Buber, 1965, p. 35). Those who withhold themselves cannot fully participate in community because that attitude prevents them from entering into genuine relation with their fellow members. May (1994) states: "I am very concerned about art educators' voice, place, identity, and sense of human agency in institutional structures that often restrict and isolate us, rather than bind us together in supportive, proactive, professional communities" (p. 134).

A genuine community is made up of "living units of relation" (Buber, 1965, p. 201). The greater community can only be as strong as the individual relationships that bind its members together. Buber (1965) claims: "What is peculiarly characteristic of the human world is above all that something takes place between one being and another the like of which can be found nowhere in nature" (p. 203). It is this "something that takes place between one being and another" that forms the building blocks of genuine community. If these building blocks are non-existent or deformed, a real or lasting community structure will not be possible.

## Social Reconstruction and Community

In recent years there have been flurries of interest and activity within the fields of general education and art education related to the establishment of "communities" and partnerships. It seems that the word, "community," as it is commonly defined, is being attached more and more often to a wide variety of group identities. While listening or watching the news on radio or TV, one is likely to hear references being made to all sorts of communities (e.g., the military community, the scientific community, the retirement community, the medical community). These "special interest groups" organize themselves around a set of common or shared concerns, beliefs, values, characteristics, and/or interests as "communities of sameness" (Hicks, 1994, p. 150). In addition, special interest groups (i.e., such "communities") often seek to lobby and/or advocate for some sort of special notice or consideration. Although not always the case, such activities are sometimes done at the expense of the general good.

Community-related concerns in art education literature have generally centered around a lack of emphasis in American culture on the unique contributions made to it by segments of its highly diversified population. As a direct result, a number of special interest groups have begun to spring up within art education's professional associations and organizations. To their credit, each of these groups seeks to call attention to some particular issue or concern that perhaps should be addressed by the whole, some area in which they feel professional knowledge should be expanded and/or professional practice developed. The philosophical underpinnings of many of these groups are purportedly those of social reconstruction, indeed, their members are often visibly active advocates for that cause within the field of art education (see for example: Blandy, 1994; Freedman, 1994a; 1994b; Hicks, 1994; May, 1994; Stuhr, 1994). Social reconstructionists in art education, advocating for increased attention to issues of multiculturalism, gender, and inclusion, for example, comprise several groups whose messages are most frequently encountered in current literature. How are we as a professional community being affected?

## Multiculturalism, Gender, Inclusion

A few years ago, at an annual conference of the National Art Education Association, Chapman (1993) spoke very briefly as a panel member on the subject of "multiculturalism" as one of the field's most promising future directions. In her remarks, she emphasized the pitfalls of teaching about a particular culture or subculture without also approaching it from and fitting it into the perspective of global culture. Teaching about, for instance, the artistic traditions of the Zuni, dissociated from the contributions Zuni traditions make to the larger American culture and/or world culture, and viewed apart from those cultural perspectives, can render such information and experience totally meaningless to students. Separated from its global links, Zuni culture does not become an interesting and enlightening instance of diversity, capable of enlarging our national or worldwide sense of self and community, but rather a mere oddity or aberration that evokes a voyeuristic mindset in those who would seek to study it.

Although it is arguably impossible for those outside a culture to gain "the emic perspective" of those within the culture (Eisner, 1994, p. 190), a posture of naturally limited participation and a role of respectful, informed observer can be achieved and, in fact, are highly preferable to that of a "cultural voyeur." Teaching from a global perspective should result in the cultivation of a sense of global community, where persons from all cultures are made dialogically welcome. That is not likely to occur if the focus of multiculturalism is continually redirected toward the inability of cultural "outsiders" to somehow meaningfully participate in or understand the signficance of beliefs and practices of a culture or subculture other than their own (Kindler, 1994).

Multicultural issues must be carefully and sensitively handled in the classroom, to avoid setting up a voyeuristic and/or tokenistic mindset (Stuhr, 1994). In their attempts to avoid marginalization of cultures, members of the art education professional community are confronted with many difficult and problematic decisions. These are not necessarily decisions about what to teach and what not to teach, as is commonly assumed, but rather, they are frequently decisions about what time, resources, and/or local mandates permit one to teach (Mims & Lankford, 1995). To press for substantial additions to the curriculum (i.e., the study of marginalized cultures and even marginalized subgroups within those cultures) (Hicks, 1994) seems somewhat ludicrous, in view of the fact that as more and more content is added, the curriculum itself becomes what is increasingly marginalized.

Gender issues have also increasingly been a source of extended discussion and extensive study within art education in recent years (Freedman, 1994b). It could be said that the field is attempting to "make up for lost time" by its rather sudden burst of attention to the painfully and embarrassingly obvious omission of women (as well as others) from the canon of art history. Those in the social reconstructionist camp who seek to redress that situation often appear to want more than appropriate amends for a "sin of omission" and seek to go beyond it in an attempt to somehow penalize or chastise artists from the past for their "sins of commission" (i.e., for earlier portrayals of the female form in a manner that is currently considered unacceptable and/or demeaning or excluding the work of women artists from serious consideration) (Freedman, 1994b). Giving women their just due in the annals of art history and within current fields of artistic endeavor is a praiseworthy goal for members of a genuine community. Reaching into the past to assail male artists and patrons for having freely followed their own artistic visions and the trends of the historical contexts in which they lived and worked (even if the end results could be construed today as "sexist imagery") could be considered a rather narrow-minded, *ex post facto* abridgement of artistic license and an absurd form of censorship. Such events can be essentially divisive-they single out a segment or segments of the population for criticism and, perhaps, censure. They clearly seem to be more indicative of the presence of collectivism, rather than of genuine community. Voluntary patronage and advocacy, or the pronounced lack of them, on the part of morally responsible individuals seems to be one equitable means for indicating personal approval or disapproval in both the art world and the educational world (Efland, 1990). That approach also seems to be the most viable way to maintain overall integrity and cohesion within art education's professional community.

Inclusion, or the education of disabled students within the regular classroom, is another social reconstuctionist issue that has continued to gain attention within the fields of general education and art education (Blandy, 1994; Willis, 1994a; 1994b). Ideally, including those with varying disabilities in the regular classroom setting seems the only moral thing to do. Isolating the two groups from each other during their formative years can set the stage for a variety of problems in an adult society. However, within many classroom settings, it is not clear that inclusion is a wholly satisfactory solution to the education of either group of students.

It has always been difficult for one teacher to be all things to all students within his or her crowded classroom (Eisner, 1994). Based on what is known about educating the emotionally, physically, visually, auditorially, perceptually, and/or mentally challenged student, good teaching often involves a substantial amount of time devoted to working more closely and slowly, using specially adapted methods and tools, repeating steps and instructions, offering extra encouragement, and/or measuring progress in smaller increments. In educating learners with special needs the demands made on teachers may be different in kind; however, the amount of time expended per student in the classroom should remain equal. Accordingly, current educational practice may make the notion of inclusion seem logistically impossible for the average art classroom and teacher. While no one with any sensitivity would argue against the aesthetic education of the disabled any more than they would for any other group, we must ask ourselves: in the long run, are the larger social outcomes more important to realize than the educational ones? If we focus less on educational outcomes, will we not be irreparably damaging society in the process? In the past, this issue has clearly demonstrated its powerful potential to divide the professional education community and move it toward collectivity. As art educators, we continue to be affected.

## Conclusion

In each of the three instances mentioned earlier (multiculturalism, gender, inclusion), "the reconstruction of society" poses several troubling dilemmas for our professional community of art educators. In light of many of the divisive approaches taken, it might even be argued that the long-term effects of each of these issues on our sense of community has the potential to be more socially deconstructive than reconstructive in nature. Any emphasis on diversity, considered apart from or at the expense of unity, can have a decidedly fragmenting effect on community. The end result can be a gradual downhill slide into a collective, where once there was genuine community. Community is where open dialogue occurs between (and among) members and leaders, not where one group dominates or constantly pushes its own interests to the forefront. Eisner (1994) maintains: "The denial of complexity, in any area of social life, is the beginning of tyranny. Those who know precisely what other people should be doing often leave no space for diversity or for debate" (p. 189).

Raging debates over issues such as these are not necessarily unhealthy events for our professional community, rather, they are indicative, according to Buber (1965), of "...a community struggling for its own reality as a community" (p. 31). However, those of our membership who advocate a new professional focus which essentially seeks to address social issues via art, appear also to be advocating a rather radical philosophical foreclosure on our more traditional primacy of focus (i.e., on the education and development of aesthetic sensibilities) (Eisner, 1994). A primary focus on social issues would seem to constitute a reductionistic approach to the teaching of art, prompting one to wonder along with Eisner, "...whether in the end art education will become little more than a handmaiden to the social studies" (Eisner, 1994, p. 190). Room for differences can be found within a genuine community, but not within a collective.

In the end, those caught up in a collective will experience "a great dissatisfaction" and become disillusioned with its "false realization of community" (Buber, 1965, p. 202). Their expectations will be unmet, they will grow weary of the isolation and restrictions they have endured. They will feel that "something important and irreplaceable" has been lost to them (p. 115). When a substantial portion of the membership of a collective reaches that point, the organizational structure will eventually collapse. Those of us within the field of art education must reevaluate our professional organizations, in an effort to prevent the gradual erosion and deterioration of genuine community. New voices and ideas must continue to be heard, enduring traditions must continue to be respected, creative opportunities for individual participation and contribution must continue to be expanded, collaboration at all levels must continue to be encouraged, the open-mindedness and "aesthetic responsibility" of the individual must continue to prevail.

Buber (1965) leaves us with the thought that, rather than being deliberately organized, planned and constructed, genuine communities happen. That does not mean that the members of a community do not play active roles in its work and structure. On the contrary, it suggests that where a genuine spirit of community exists and thrives and where each member retains his/her voice, sense of identity and responsibility within the whole, the welfare of the group and the individuals within the group, is best served. "Community is where community happens" (p. 31). Collectivity happens where the individual's identity becomes lost in that of the dominating crowd, where there is no genuine dialogue "between" members and leaders, where the desires or causes of one group are promoted at the expense of others, or where competition and self-serving attitudes are present. Collectivity requires the surrender of self; genuine community requires the pledge of self. Let us, as art educators, pledge our "selves" anew to developing and maintaining genuine community within our professional organizations and chosen field of endeavor.

# References

Blandy, D. (1994). Assuming responsibility: Disability rights and the preparation of art teachers. *Studies in Art Education, 35*(3), 179-187.

Buber, M. (1958). *I and thou.* (Trans. R. G. Smith.). New York: Scribner's.

Buber, M. (1965). *Between man and man.* New York: Collier Books.

Chapman, L. H., Hausman, J. J., Eisner, E. W., & Feldman, E. B. (1993). Our best advice and counsel to art teachers: 1993. In *NAEA Distinguished Fellows Forum.* Panel discussion at the annual meeting of the National Art Education Association, Chicago, IL.

Clark-Winright, E. R. (1991). M. Buber's *I and thou* as model for relationship between artist and visual artwork. (Doctoral dissertation, Texas Tech University). *Dissertation Abstracts International, 57,* 3507A.

Dowrick, S. (1991). *Intimacy and solitude: Balancing closeness and independence.* New York: W. W. Norton.

Efland, A. D. (1990). *A history of art education: Intellectual and social currents in teaching the visual arts.* New York: Teachers College Press.

Eisner, E. W. (1994). Revisionism in art education: Some comments on the preceding articles. *Studies in Art Education, 35*(3), 188-191.

Freedman, K. (1994a). About this issue: The social reconstruction of art education. *Studies in Art Education, 35*(3), 131-134.

Freedman, K. (1994b). Interpreting gender and visual culture in art classrooms. *Studies in Art Education, 35*(3), 157-170.

Hicks, L. E. (1994). Social reconstruction and community. *Studies in Art Education, 35*(3), 149-156.

Kindler, A. M. (1994). Children and the culture of a multicultural society. *Art Education, 47*(4), 54-60.

May, W. T. (1994). The tie that binds: Reconstructing ourselves in institutional contexts. *Studies in Art Education, 35*(3), 135-148.

Mims, S. K., & Lankford, E. L. (1995). Time, money, and the new art education: A nationwide investigation. *Studies in Art Education, 36*(2), 84-95.

Stuhr, P. L. (1994). Multicultural art education and social reconstruction. *Studies in Art Education, 35*(3), 171-178.

Willis, S. (1994a, October). Making schools more inclusive: Teaching children with disabilities in regular classrooms. *Curriculum Update.* Alexandria, VA: Association for Supervision and Curriculum Development.

Willis, S. (1994b, October). Inclusion and the disruptive child. *Curriculum Update.* Alexandria, VA: Association for Supervision and Curriculum Development.

# Hawaii: Arts Education Partnerships in A Diverse Community

Peggy Hunt
*University of Hawaii at Manoa*

The Hawaiian Islands include diverse cultural communities, extremely varied art forms and a multitude of organizations promoting arts education. Partnerships, networking and communication are common in this small and insular location, and the arts are a cherished part of each culture and the common culture. In this context, where per capita funding for the arts has been one of the highest in the United States, arts education has a unique profile. Although school children in Hawaii are exposed to a wide variety of artwork and performances, there are few art educators in the schools. Unique partnerships among the Hawaii Alliance for Arts Education, The Department of Education, The State Foundation on Culture and the Arts, professional performance companies, and the University of Hawaii at Manoa (hereafter 'the University') provide a model for community networking in arts education. The diversity of cultures (14-20 different ethnic groups) in the schools and community serves as a springboard for communication in arts education. Although strong cultural identity can tend to isolate ethnic cultural groups, involvement in arts activities can serve as a bridge and a way to celebrate the diversity and commonality among cultures.

The place of the arts in Hawaii today is due in large part to the indigenous Hawaiian culture, in which every aspect of life is imbued with art and artmaking. Thus, despite the many waves of immigrants, the art of each tradition has been accepted as part of the larger "local" culture. With this comes the spirit of *kama'aina* which means being local, "belonging to the land," being part of the island community. *Kama'aina* includes all people who live inside this multifaceted, multiracial, multicultural society, and their cultural traditions. Many of the partnerships found in the art community are possible due to an inclusive rather than an exclusive spirit of *kama'aina*. This leads to multicultural art forms and to a cooperative relationship among many artists and arts organizations.

In traditional Hawaiian culture the boundaries between music, dance, theatre, and art are fluid. This is true in many indigenous societies; the sacred, the secular, arts, and education are not separate but serve each other and the culture. The traditional Hawaiian hula and chant combines history lessons, cosmology, lineage, moral codes, navigational wisdom, art, dance, song, and theatrical revue. Hula is also the sacred, the ritual, and the blessing. To separate the sacred from art or pluck the aesthetic from knowledge is relatively new in human history and very Eurocentric. In contrast, the indigenous culture of Hawaii continues to set the tone for the current place of the arts in these islands. The integrated nature of Hawaiian culture is often exemplified as a *lei*, a necklace of plaited flowers in which all the parts connect with each other and form a whole. The *lei* also provides a metaphor for the different peoples, cultures and traditions strung together in Hawaii.

As all elements of life were integrated for ancient Hawaiians, so this spirit extended to each wave of immigrants. Commonly used Hawaiian words exemplify this spirit of integration, wholeness, acceptance, and respect:

*Aloha*: love, mercy, compassion, pity, greeting, loved one to love.

*Kama'aina*: native-born host, acquainted, familiar.

*Ohana*: family, relative, kin group, related.

*Kuleana*: right, title, property, responsibility, jurisdiction.

The prominence of these words mirrors the value placed on relationship, individual responsibility and jurisdiction-a wonderful base for partnerships. The Hawaiian language and the image of the *lei* demonstrate the "welcomeness" of this environment for arts partnerships. In fact the high level of collaboration and partnerships in the arts could almost be seen as endemic to Hawaii.

The island vocabulary provides insight for understanding this ethnically diverse culture. The word *hapa*, used with affection, means "part," or a person of mixed blood. Although a mixed ethnicity is scorned in many cultures, in Hawaii *hapa* is as much a part of the culture as a *lei* with carnations and orchids, and is embraced and celebrated. Politicians proudly run as *hapa*; it is a title of belonging, and it definitely makes one "local" and *kama'aina*. *Hapa* children and grandchildren have opened divergent cultures to becoming a part of the *lei* of populations in Hawaii. The spirit of *hapa*, combined with love for the arts and cooperation, has spawned many arts consortiums and art forms that reflect the multicultural reality in Hawaii.

From the first contact with outside peoples, the culture of Hawaii has integrated new elements into its "local" culture. Each group of people coming to the islands brought their distinctive foods, language, religion, music, dances, theatre, and visual arts. Hawaii's location has attracted immigrants from a wide range of locations, the majority being Asian, with Caucasians and Polynesians (including Hawaiian natives) as significant minorities. In Hawaii the words *ethnic* and *ethnicity* are common usage on every official document, whether a driver's license application, the intake form at a doctor's office, or the Department of Education's (DOE) enrollment statistics. These words define categories formed at intersections of race, ethnicity, and culture. These categories do not correspond to academic definitions of ethnicity and do not consistently emphasize either race or ethnic ancestry. For example, alongside "Caucasian" we find "Portuguese," "Malaysian," and "African-American" census designations. A typical public school encompasses 14 different ethnic groups, likely to include the following: Filipino, Chinese, Japanese, Samoan, Micronesian, Polynesian, Korean, Vietnamese, Cambodian, Thai, Okinawan, Hawaiian, African-American, Portuguese, Puerto Rican, Mexican, Indonesian, Malaysian, Caucasian. (Figure 1 documents the ethnicity of entering freshman students at the University of Hawaii at Manoa for Fall 1996.)

Figure 1

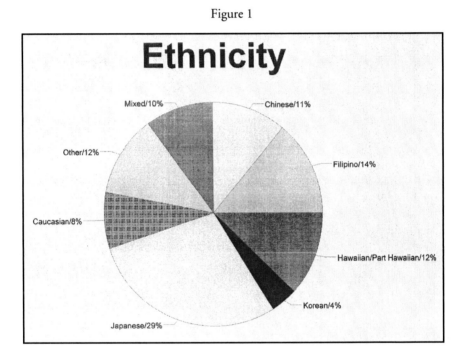

The population in Hawaii is not primarily representative of the Western, Eurocentric culture that informs much of the art and art education of the United States and Canada, but is a very diverse Asian/Polynesian cultural mix. This is not to diminish the heightened influence of American culture in every part of the globe, but to emphasize the strong cultural differences between Hawaii and the rest of the United States. In Hawaii, every ethnic group's cultural arts are an integral part of the common culture and thus a visible reminder of the individual cultural groups that exist in Hawaii. In any given week, one might partake of a(n) Hawaiian hula, chant, song, ukulele or slack key guitar concert; Japanese taiko drumming, kabuki, butoh, or noh theatre; Balinese dance or theatre; Javanese gamelon concert or shadow puppets; Korean dance, music, or mask performance;

Chinese Beijing Opera, lion dance, or orchestra concert; Okinawan dance and music; Afro-Caribbean drumming; Philippine dance; or "local" theatre in pidgin, to name only a few of the performing arts that are available. The visual arts reflect this diversity of cultures and are everywhere apparent, along with the abundant presence of public sculpture.

In addition to these individual cultural art forms, the partnering and blending between Asian, Pacific, European, and other traditions produces many "crossover" and "fusion" forms. All the arts blend, consort, exist side by side, and support each other. University students in theatre have directed "Asian-fusion" plays, in which techniques from Beijing Opera and butoh are set to Shakespearean dialogue to make a new form, pieces in which the culturally distinctive methods sparkle like jewels in an original setting. Similarly, "World Beat" music blends a wide variety of rhythmic styles, as typified by the Hawaii an group *Cabasake*, whose motto "many tribes, one village" describes this genre of music and the diversity of these musicians. *Cabasake* brings together a Japanese taiko drummer, a black Brazilian percussionist, a "local" jazz/rock keyboard player, a Portuguese playing African drums, and an African-American jazz guitarist. Each artist brings a unique musical tradition, plays with his/her own voice, and produces harmony in this "one village." Just as being *hapa* is valued as a common, accepted, and prestigious state of human ethnicity, *hapa* is also a positive force in the arts.

*Hula,* the indigenous dance form, has many incarnations that reflect the acceptance of changes in the total culture. A hula concert often features ancient hula— sacred and expressionless dancers in *ki*-leaf skirts, accompanied with drum and chant-along with more commercial-looking hulas performed by dancers in high-necked Victorian dresses, high heels, and smiling faces, accompanied by amplified guitar and song. As the hula has increased its repertoire with changing times, so the visual arts of Hawaii have changed and mingled with other traditions in painting, wood carving, pottery, and printmaking.

In this small, diverse cultural community in which sharing, celebrating, and harmonizing within the arts and ethnic communities is common, it is not surprising that many partnerships have sprung up between arts and arts education organizations. The physical and cultural isolation of these islands, along with a lack of art education and art teachers in the schools, has increased the need for partnerships. Although the arts are cherished, arts education for everyone is not prioritized and funded by the State Department of Education. However, what the public schools lack, the private schools have. Hawaii has the third highest private school enrollment in the United States, and the fine art programs in these schools are well funded. Still, the public schools, which serve most of the 800,000 people on the island of Oahu, employ only a few arts teachers: five drama teachers, one after-school dance program, two choral teachers, visual arts teachers in only 8% of the schools and a "fairly decent" number of band programs. The juxtaposition of a large, diverse arts community and an understaffed "poor," arts education program has led to a large number of interesting partnerships in Hawaii.

As a result, school children in Hawaii are exposed to a wide variety of artwork and performances through numerous partnerships among the Hawaii Alliance for Arts Education (HAAE), the Department of Education (DOE), the State Foundation for Culture and the Arts (SFCA), the University and a myriad of professional performance companies and art venues. The diversity, richness, and multitude of artists and arts organizations presenting education activities in Hawaii is quite overwhelming. The following is a short list of the most active and most consistently funded (by the SFCA) of these: Alliance for Drama Education, Hawaii Youth Symphony, Very Special Arts Hawaii, Honolulu Theatre for Youth, Hawaii Opera Theatre, Dance as We Dance, Creative Movement in the Schools, Honolulu Printmaking Workshop, The Contemporary Museum, Hui Noeau, The Honolulu Arts Academy, Hawaii Video Curriculum Association, Hawaii Youth Opera Chorus and Poets in the Schools. Other groups, such as Artists in the Schools (funded by the DOE); the State Libraries and Parks and Recreation Department; and the University, also offer programs for children.

How so many groups cooperate to provide so much for children goes back to the Hawaiian words *ohana* and *kuleana*, which describe being part of one family by respecting the responsibility and jurisdiction of each member. Clark discusses these same phenomena as "the genuine community" in which the individual "pledges personal responsibility for decisive action and meaningful involvement" to the community (Clark, see Chapter 2). This allows for individual relationships in which: "There is present a sense of genuine respect, trust, collegiality, mutuality of purpose, and wholehearted acceptance of differences" (Clark, see Chapter 2). In Hawaii the arts community provides many examples of Clark's ideal and *ohana* and *kuleana*. There are rich performance partnerships between Honolulu Theatre for Youth and Very Special Arts Hawaii that use special populations in theatre productions. Personnel and resources are shared by Alliance for Drama Education, the University Theatre Department, Kuma Kahua Theatre and Honolulu Theatre for Youth, all while serving the schoolchildren of Hawaii. "Local" playwrights might include parts for Chinese dragon dancers or Hawaiian hula dancers, and sponsorship could span a number of theatre and cultural organizations. Dancers teach in the Creative Movement in the Schools program and perform with *Dances We Dance* as they collaborate with the University dance program in a shared concert. Resources are pooled, personnel is shared, diversity is celebrated, and a huge amount of experience with the arts is channeled into the schools. This is not the incestuous interplay of a clique or elite group but rather the organic, healthy flow of a large community and a model for "genuine community."

Statewide organizations support the arts education community and its partnerships. The SFCA gives arts education partnership grants ($42,600 in 1996) where there is a commitment at the school level to infuse the arts into the educational process. The HAAE, as a statewide group, has as one of its goals fostering partnerships among arts organizations, and between the schools and community arts. HAAE's membership covers a wide range of artists, educators, arts organizations and representatives from the SFCA and the DOE, whose facilities serve as a meeting ground and networking center for those interested in art education. The Artists in the Schools program, sponsored by the DOE, is one of the oldest in the United States and schedules artists and arts educators to give residencies in the schools. This program works in partnerships with HAAE, SFCA and the rest of the DOE to promote arts education in the public schools.

The arts and arts education partnerships are alive and well in Hawaii and tens of thousands of children are interfacing with the arts this year because of it. The smooth interweaving of all of these groups, their partnerships and networking, are possible because of *ohana* and the spirit of *kama'aina*, with acknowledgment of *kuleana*. While the fact that so many can work so well together to make this happen is a tribute to the local culture and the reality of *ohana*, it is nevertheless an incomplete solution to the small arts education budget. The $42,600 art education budget of the State Foundation for Culture and the Arts would not even fund two regular art teachers. This money, in partnership with other funding sources, brings short-term art experiences to a large number of schools. Yet the wonderful experiences provided by the network of artists and arts organizations do not replace the need for full-time art educators in the schools. The challenge facing the art education community is to help schools make arts education a priority in three ways:

1) Inviting artists to come into the schools.
2) Providing inservice training in the arts for classroom teachers.
3) Having arts educators in each of the arts on staff to consult with teachers and give specialized classes.

The first of these goals is being accomplished through art partnerships. The second and third goals are moving ahead through work by the HAAE, SFCA, and the DOE. The most effective way to accomplish these goals will be with partnerships, which bring educators, community members, and arts educators together. Using the *aloha* spirit to build on the partnerships forged by the arts community, an awareness of the importance of arts education for all children continues to grow in Hawaii.

## Endnote

The discussion in this article focuses primarily on the island of Oahu, home to 800,000 of the one million inhabitants of Hawaii, and on Honolulu, the urban, political, and cultural center of the state and area responsible for most arts initiatives and presenters. The information has come from a wide variety of publications and interviews, and as a participant observer in Hawaii's arts and arts education community.

## References

Hawaii Alliance for Arts Education. (1993-1996). *Minutes.* Honolulu.

Hawaii State Foundation of Culture and the Arts. (1993-1996). *Annual Report.* Honolulu.

Oppenheimer, S. (1995). *Performing arts in education in Hawaii: A history of drama, puppetry, and creative movement for children and youth from 1875-1994.* Dissertation, University of Hawaii at Manoa.

University of Hawaii. (1993-1996). *Ku Lama.* University of Hawaii: Office of the Vice President for University Relations.

# Commonwealth Games, Showcase for Visual Art

Robert Dalton
*University of Victoria*

To some extent the value of art education is linked to the value we place upon art. When the visual arts are seen as making a significant contribution to the life of a community, it becomes easier for art teachers to argue for the importance of educating the young about art, and providing the time and resources needed to support a strong curriculum in public school education. Effective advocacy for art education must then include educating the public about art and the vital role it plays in social life.

All around us we can see examples of the contributions of artists—the work of architects, interior designers, industrial designers, graphic designers, and fine artists enhances our lives in many ways. But from time to time there are special occasions when art has an opportunity to play a particularly prominent role. The XV Commonwealth Games held in Victoria, British Columbia, in 1994 was one such occasion. It brought into partnership sports and the arts. In this complex mingling of athletic events, exhibitions, and performances, the arts gave much and gained much. This case study investigates the participation of the arts in general and visual art in particular within the XV Commonwealth Games. It looks at the nature and scope of the contributions made by art, the organizational structure, the partnerships and alliances that made it all possible, and the legacy. That legacy includes the benefits for art education. The data have been gathered primarily from newspaper reports about the events. Extensive media coverage in Victoria's daily newspaper and publications from the Commonwealth Games Society informed the public as to the plans and progress of the Games and the Cultural Festival that accompanied it.

## The Commonwealth Games

The British Commonwealth comprises approximately one third of the world's population. Over 64 countries and territories were represented at the Games, from places as large and populous as India to places as small as the Falkland Islands. The Games are held every 4 years, the previous site being Auckland, New Zealand. The

1998 Games were held in Kuala Lumpur, Malaysia. Planning for the Victoria Games began in 1987 when Victoria won out over nine other Canadian cities vying for the honor. The 1994 Games marked the return of South Africa, excluded since 1958 due to its apartheid policy. They also marked the final appearance of Hong Kong, returned to China in 1997 when Britain's lease expired. In all 3,345 athletes participated in the various events which ranged from pole vault to swimming, and from weightlifting to lawn bowling. Funding for the Games and related activities called for a budget of approximately $160 million—$100 million coming from various levels of government, $143 million from corporate sponsors and rights holders, and $37 million from ticket sales.

The political significance of the Games cannot be ignored. Present to officially open the Games was Queen Elizabeth accompanied by Prince Philip and Prince Edward. Canada's Prime Minister, Jean Chretien stated that "All Canadians have interests and investments at stake in the XV Commonwealth Games" (Kieran, 1994, p. 3). Political agendas were many and varied. Unity among Commonwealth members was emphasized and nationalism was apparent as athletes competed under their respective flags. It was also an occasion for recognition of Canada's indigenous people. The Games recognized disabled athletes who competed in events such as the wheelchair race. Each day an estimated 700,000 to 1.2 million people around the globe watched television coverage of the Commonwealth Games; the opening ceremonies were seen by an audience estimated to be between 300 and 500 million television viewers worldwide. For a brief period there was an intensely bright spotlight trained on the city of Victoria, British Columbia.

## Showcase for Culture and Visual Art

"The XV Commonwealth Games is an international athletic competition that promotes opportunities for human development and celebrates cross-cultural understanding, the tradition of good sportsmanship, and the triumph of personal achievement" (Kieran, 1994, p. 2). In this statement published by the Victoria Commonwealth Games Society, it is evident that the Games are more than a sporting event. Athletic competition, by itself, could not achieve all the goals of the Games. "Celebrating cross-cultural understanding" is a goal more effectively achieved by the showcase for culture that took place in conjunction with the Games. Through dance, music, costume, exhibitions, and demonstrations of artwork, those in attendance were able to experience elements of the cultural richness and diversity of the Commonwealth.

First Nations groups from Vancouver Island played a major part in the festivities. The Lekwammen people of the Coast Salish acted as the First Nations host at the Games. For the Lekwammen this was an occasion to restore traditional culture and to build spiritual and emotional bridges to their people and non-Natives. They held their first *potlatch* since such events were banned in 1884 (Tanner, 1987); that traditional celebration, marking special occasions with feasts and gift giving, had been regarded by missionaries as pagan and by paternalistic legislators as excessively lavish. In 1951, the potlatch law was quietly dropped from the Indian Act. Guests came to the Lekwammen potlatch by canoe from the Pacific Northwest; a flotilla of approximately 30 cedar vessels, including large whaling and war canoes was welcomed in traditional manner. A cultural village was established with Native crafts, demonstrations of traditional Native sports, and other activities. Marking the occasion too, was the dedication of the world's tallest totem pole, a joint venture involving carvers from the three Nations of Vancouver Island.

Among the many functions of art is "making special" (Dissanayake, 1988). The opening and closing ceremonies were indeed made special by the contribution of art. An important symbol was the Queen's Baton which held her opening address. Bearing Native designs and carved in the shape of a soul-catcher, the Baton was transported from London to Port Rupert on the northern tip of Vancouver Island and from there it traveled south by canoe, finally being carried to the stadium by runner and First Nations athlete Angela Chalmers. Elaborate sets were constructed for various aspects of the opening ceremonies that included a Native creation legend involving monumental articulated puppets. Costumes, banners, and other visual works added much to the spectacle involving 4,000 volunteer performers and lasting 2 hours. One of the more unique aspects of the closing ceremonies was the display of an enormous fabric artwork called the "Commonwealth Cape of Many Hands." The work was composed of hands traced from people of all Commonwealth countries and required the efforts of 225 needleworkers to stitch this cape. The Games became a spectacle through the involvement of numerous artists. The distinctive logo of the Games was displayed on advertisements and banners throughout the city. Present to provide the public with a visual record of events was another group of artists, 275 photographers. From the design of the $22 million Commonwealth Pool to the tiny trading pins, and from Klee Wyck, the killer whale mascot to pyrotechnic artist Navarro's fireworks, art and the contributions of artists were everywhere.

Away from the Games venues there were craft fairs, one displaying the work of artists from Commonwealth countries. Another, the "First Peoples Festival" featured the work of Native artists. Also endorsed by the Festival, "Artisans '94" showed the work of local craftspersons. Most of the visual artists whose work was shown at the Games Festival were Canadian. Fine art exhibitions such as "Markings" displayed work by British Columbia artists. "Arts from the Arctic" was an exhibition of work from the Canadian Arctic and from other circumpolar regions—Siberia, Greenland, Alaska, and Arctic Scandinavia. Augmenting this was an exhibition of monumental sculptures being carved at an open-air site. Inuit artists at work on whale bone and massive limestone blocks, West Coast Native artists carving cedar, and other demonstrations generated considerable interest among visitors and local people who gathered to watch. In order to use all available spaces for exhibiting, artworks were also displayed in store windows and doorways. "Window Watching" made use of donated spaces in retail stores and vacant properties, becoming a walking tour of visual art displays. Victoria residents received a special newspaper from *The Works* that promoted the various shows. *Eye to Eye* provided readers with a map identifying sites, photographs of representative artworks, descriptions of the shows, and other information of use to anyone interested in viewing art.

Months before the Games began there were major arts events in anticipation of the Games. An international conference was organized by an alternative gallery in Victoria; participants examined issues related to the theme "Mined Cultures: Contemporary Artists and Post-Colonialism in the Commonwealth." Connected with this was "Independents' Day," a festival of experimental, narrative, documentary, animation films, and short videos hosted by Victoria colleges, galleries, and museums. The festival sampled films and videos which reflect the identity and spirit of Commonwealth peoples. "A World Beyond Borders" was the theme of the annual Canadian Conference of the Arts. It dealt with topics such as cultural sovereignty and the survival of aboriginal cultures in the electronic revolution. "Palindrome: Commonwealth Artists Exchange" was a program where Victoria artists hosted artists from Britain and Australia; those visits were reciprocated the following year.

## Organizing the Arts and Cultural Activities

A venture like this requires considerable planning. The Cultural Festival involved approximately 500 artists and arts organizations, and lasted from July 15 through August 28, much longer than the 10-day Commonwealth Games. Partnerships were formed to manage the complex arrangements and administer the $300,000 budget allotted to this important part of the Games. Two coordinating bodies were engaged: The Native Participation Committee, and The Works. The former was engaged to involve First Nations Peoples at the highest level of decision making. Their knowledge, contacts, and support were essential. The Works was organized by the Alberta Part Art Society, a nonprofit organization that strives to advance the visual arts in Canada. The society had a successful history of organizing international arts festivals.

The decision to engage a group from outside British Columbia when capable people were here and willing to take on the assignment was controversial. An established and experienced group was finally awarded the responsibility because it was considered better able to gain the confidence of government, thereby guaranteeing adequate funding. Still, this was something of a lost legacy. As a result of this decision, Victoria lost an opportunity to develop expertise that could have proved valuable in years to come.

## The Legacy of the Games and the Cultural Festival

It may be easier to discuss the legacy of the Games than that of the Cultural Festival. Sports facilities, housing for athletes, an endowment to foster sports in Victoria; these are tangible ways of measuring the benefits to local sports organizations. No such material legacy, however, was left to arts groups. But in attempting to assess the positive impact of the Cultural Festival, one might begin by discussing audiences. As part of the Festival, free nightly concerts known as "Harborfest" were a huge success, at least if one can judge by attendance figures. Cultural groups from Tonga, Jamaica, Australia, and Zimbabwe entertained crowds. There was music to suit various tastes, from symphony orchestras and concert bands, to popular performers who drew the largest audiences. Harborfest may actually have eclipsed the Games in attendance and enthusiasm. The minister responsible for the Games described the Festival as hugely successful, with attendence estimated at 70,000.

Audiences at visual arts exhibitions are not so easily measured, especially when those exhibits may be seen from the street, all day long. For at least one venue, estimates were available; approximately 60,000 people saw "Arts from the Arctic." But numbers, impressive as they may seem, do not tell the whole story. While only 100 participants were expected to attend the conference on Mined Cultures, this does not mean the conference was unsuccessful. A small yet influential group can be profoundly affected by the proceedings and contacts made at a conference, while large numbers may soon forget an exhibition. Determining the impact of the Cultural Festival is beyond the scope of this report but it does raise important questions about assessing the educational value of events such as this.

## A Unique Partnership

Sport and art are not common partners. What were the benefits of such a union? It seems reasonable to conclude that art made a significant contribution to the XV Commonwealth Games. Art was everywhere and was present in many forms, helping to create a sense of excitement. Together, sport and art were able to attract larger audiences than either one alone. Certainly in a city known for tourism, attracting visitors is important, but beyond the practical advantages of the partnership, how might the public image of sport and art be enhanced by association? For sports, the Games becomes something more than sweat and muscle; allied with art, sport gains a sense of refinement and beauty, even intellectual pursuit. Art gains as well; there is a feeling of youth, vigor, and discipline which may be associated with these world class athletes.

If we accept that the union, however temporary, was mutually beneficial, we might then ask how integrated or alike the two should become. The Festival emphasized the art of Canada. We might ask whether Commonwealth countries should be equally represented in arts events as they are in sport. Disabled athletes participated in the Games but were given no such profile in any art exhibition. Should they be? Gender division was an obvious aspect of the sports competitions. Does this have a place in art exhibitions? Competition for gold, silver, and bronze medals is central to the Games. Would it be desirable to promote a more competitive spirit among artists? First Nations people played a major role in the cultural events surrounding the games but were much less visible as Games athletes. Should this be a concern? Clearly there are differences in the way art and sports events are organized. Perhaps an ideal partnership is one in which there is a complementary relationship, one that respects the unique contribution of each partner. New understandings and further liaison may result from thoughtfully constructed relationships.

## Art Education and Advocacy

There was wide exposure for art at the Commonwealth Games but how educational was this exposure? Exposure is only a beginning; the role of an art educator is to mediate, to make the most of the opportunity to teach. It is entirely possible that the public may fail to recognize the full extent of the contribution of art to an event like the Commonwealth Games. And the public may be bewildered as they gaze upon an avant garde artwork which supposedly "speaks for itself." Educators are needed to guide viewers in recognizing the breadth and depth of art, and its meaning in other cultures. This may take place before, during, and after the actual events. There were specific initiatives where the focus was more evidently educational. Prior to the Games, students from Cowichan Secondary School created a ceramic mural that was installed at the track and field venue. In doing this project, students learned about art, the Commonwealth, and the sporting events of the Games. Yet another example of art education can be seen when the Lekwammen learned more about their heritage through the carving of the Spirit of the Nations pole, the potlatch, and other cultural events. There were other initiatives as well, ones that followed the Games. The Canadian Broadcasting Corporation co-sponsored "Spirit of the Arctic," a film based on the monumental Arctic art shown at the Games. It must be remembered that art education is not confined to public school classrooms. Art exhibitions may be highly educational. When visitors stop to watch an artist at work, read published statements about artwork, and listen as artists discuss issues of importance to them, art education is taking place.

While we may accept that art education occurred during and following the Games, it is a leap to assume that this translates into wide support for art and for art education. And yet the question is a significant one: To what extent do such events contribute to advocacy for art education? Much of the literature dealing with advocacy embraces a rather narrow definition of art education. Mittler and Stinespring (1991) define art education advocacy as efforts made to underscore the educational values of school art programs, effectively answering the question: Why should the visual arts be taught in our nation's schools? Normally, such campaigns involve lists of benefits that accrue to those who take art education courses. Finely crafted rationales have been prepared by groups of art educators at the national level, provincial or state level, and local level. Writers of art curricula often begin with statements about the value of art education, as do writers of textbooks intended to prepare university students to teach art. Strong support for the value of art education from influential groups whose focus is normally much wider than art or education such as the National Conference of State Legislatures (Loyacono, 1992) are generally welcomed and enthusiastically disseminated, as are statements of support from prominent members of the business community.

Much of the literature is directed towards bringing pressure to bear on the decisionmakers. It is aimed at the top. Bruhn (1994) describes advocacy as half persuasion and half politics. Converts must be won and persuaded to act, brilliant strategies must be devised, and participants must be taught how to do the job of influencing the decision-makers. Lynch (1994) and others emphasize the role of partnerships in successful advocacy, coalitions of arts groups must be persuaded that it is in their interest to support art education. Educators must also unite—higher education, teachers, principals, school boards, and parent groups can be a powerful voice when united. Speaking with one voice and moving towards goals which inspire public confidence such as the setting of national standards for arts education (Consortium of National Arts Education Associations, 1994), the aims of advocacy are advanced.

Against the backdrop of these well-orchestrated campaigns, one might wonder if any support for art education was garnered at the Commonwealth Games. A showcase for visual art should cultivate an audience for art. Through demonstrating the very real contributions of art to community life, support is built for art and, by implication, for art education. It is more of a "soft sell" approach to advocacy than the sustained and more focused campaigns that are also necessary. When presented with opportunities, art educators should become involved to increase exposure for art, to assist in making the experience as educational as possible, to document what has taken place so that students and the public at large might continue to derive educational benefit after the events have concluded.

The media play an extremely important role in reporting grand scale arts events. The value of art educators developing a mutually beneficial relationship with the editors of print and broadcast media should not be underestimated. The public must be informed about events if they are to attend; interest must be captured, and the meaning and significance of the artwork must be explained. Journalists often welcome suggestions for stories and they depend on information from insiders and experts in explaining events. Rather than hoping that editors and journalists will learn about art events, art educators can become proactive, appointing representatives to serve as media liaison and spokespersons.

Not every city can attract these kinds of opportunities or funding to stage cultural festivals. Nevertheless, art educators would do well to explore possibilities for partnerships in events that may be enhanced by the contribution and showcasing of art. Seeing opportunities and making the most of them is a strategy that must be considered when we seek to build support for art education. Effective advocacy must do more than lobby politicians, it must educate the whole community. Advocacy and art education go hand in hand.

# References

Bruhn, K. (1994). Advocacy: Getting to "How to." In B. Boston (Ed.), *Perspectives on implementation: Arts education standards for America's students* (pp. 9-18). Reston, VA: Music Educators National Conference.

Consortium of National Arts Education Associations. (1994). *National standards for arts education: What every young American should know and be able to do in the arts.* Reston, VA: Music Educators National Conference.

Dissanayake, E. (1988). *What is art for?* Seattle: University of Washington Press.

Kieran, C. (Ed.). (1994). *Spirit.* Victoria Commonwealth Games Society: Victoria, British Columbia.

Loyacono, L. (1992). *Reinventing the wheel: A design for student achievement in the 2lst century.* Washington, DC: The National Conference of State Legislatures.

Lynch, R. (1994). Implementing the standards: Making use of the arts community. In B. Boston (Ed.), *Perspectives on implementation: Arts education standards for America's students* (pp. 75-81). Reston, VA: Music Educators National Conference.

Mittler, G., & Stinespring, J. (1991). Intellect, emotion, and art education. *Design for Arts in Education, 92*(6), 13-19.

Tanner, M. (1987). *The wretched giving away system is the root of all iniquity: The Missionary Society and Kwakiutl potlatches, 1878-1912.* Unpublished master's thesis, University of Victoria, British Columbia.

Watts, R. (1994, July 15). Controversial art show finds venue at theatre. *Times Colonist,* p. B1.

# School-Community Collaboration and Artistic Process

Jacques-Albert Wallot and Bruno Joyal
*Université du Québec à Montréal*

At the secondary level [students'] collective works may constitute an important component of creative activities engaged in during an academic year. Since collective works are an attempt to escape the rigidity of the secondary school curriculum time-table, art teachers are aware that most outstanding productions originate ouside the classroom. Partnerships with community services provides a natural extension of the art class. As well, medium-range objectives specified in Fine Art programs find a natural outlet in the cultural space provided by society at large.

While the school constitutes a community in itself, replete with its own values, norms, and projects, its authorities are increasingly concerned with its role through municipal services. As an active member in the community, it should offer the "shared consciousness of membership" referred to by Hicks (1994, p. 150). Students should have the opportunity to demonstrate their sense of belonging by participating in the events that punctuate the social life of the community. However, it is the art teacher—through the art class—who most often contributes to collective projects such as murals, installations, allegorical floats, and other forms of public art. In other words, social activites are often the natural outcome of an art class.

We believe collective projects provide a sense of belonging , an essential ingredient to group formation materialised in the uniqueness of the artwork. Another interesting feature stems from the fact that large groups can be involved if subdivided into smaller ones, based on a logic which borrows directly from the European art tradition of the *Atelier* of the masters and from the pedagogical structure of the art class. Other parts of the world may historically use collective experiences in artmaking. However, this chapter is limited to examples in Western art.

In discussing collective works in the art world, we must bear in mind masters such as Villard de Honnecourt (13th century), who synchronised the work of various artisan guilds, such as stone hewers, and sculptors, carpenters, tinsmiths, etc., in the construction of Notre-Dame in Paris (Erlande-Brandenburg, Pernoud, Gimpel, & Bechman, 1986); or later, Peter-Paul Rubens who, in the 17th century, orchestrated the accomplishment of the *Triumph of Marie de Medicis*; and closer in time to us, Christo, who conceived of, negotiated for, and oversaw the building of the installation *Running Fence*, from 1971 to 1976.

Within the pedagogic context, as well as in the art world, the management of collective activities is no easy feat. How does one distribute the work? How does one ensure the visual consistency of an undertaking? How does one ensure that for each student there is a balance between the collective wishes of the group and the authentic and personal contribution of the individual? The art teacher can borrow techniques from guilds and important painting ateliers, but must, at the same time, deal with the individual and unique reality of each student, all while working within the confines of a scholastic structure.

Within the context of a collective project, the necessity for the art teacher to ensure an end result that is visually coherent, while exhorting the richest possible contribution on the part of the student, is therefore, not something which will be acomplished without any difficulties. The history of art teaches us that even the greatest artists have been faced with this problem. This immediately brings to mind the story recounted by Vasari (1983) concerning the *Baptism of Christ* by Verrocchio in San Salvi. Vasari reveals that Verrocchio's young disciple, Leonardo Da Vinci, painted in one corner of the picture an angel that was more beautiful than all the rest. After Leonardo, despite his youth, had surpassed the quality of his mentor's work, Verrocchio decided never to lift a paintbrush again.

Over the past decades, the field of art education has been greatly influenced by the idea that any form of art produced by a child has to be "authentic" and result from a child's own creative potential. This notion steming from German Expressionism and later reinforced by Lowenfeld (1947), places enormous constraints upon the art teacher. The teacher cannot make a drawing or a sketch and then ask the students to enlarge it; it is inappropriate for him or her to make changes directly to students' work or even to begin a piece and let the students finish it. At the same time, art history has taught us that these particular teaching methods have in the past been used effectively: Cimabue and Giotto, among many others, proceeded in this fashion. In other cases, an artist such as Masaccio would begin a work, and Fra Fillippo Lippi would then complete it. Furthermore, in other situations, an overburdened painter such as Botticelli would request collaborators in order to finish the large number of contracts demanded of his studio.

In this respect, one thing becomes very clear: the nature of the relationship between the director of the project and the participant can unfold on one or many levels; thus, the problem of style during the era of Villard de Honnecourt appears to be of less importance. Europe, during this time, was steeped in the trend of International Gothic—the entire Western world conceived its images within the same style, where invention took refuge in alegorical metaphor, or, one might say, the ability to substitute to the text an imagery that advantageously replaces it. The individuality of the Medieval person is poorly developed when compared to our own because the subsidiary position defines medieval people as part of a collective first.

The visual model of this time, as with all others, is rigid, yet very simple. For example, the Cathedral of Chartres is covered almost entirely with column statues. This particular formal choice is sufficient to give great coherence to the entire construction.

Conversely, in the 17th century, Rubens provides a perfect illustration of the individualism which, up until then, had continued to develop, and the relations that he maintained with his apprentices were those of Master and pupil. Right from the start, the apprentice had to show an affinity for the Master since he must acquire his style and mannerisms. To acquire the right to study, he or she had to abdicate his or her own personality in favour of the Master's. It is easily understood how only strong gifted people were able to survive such conditions. It is important to note, however, that the Master would look for just such personalities in order to maximize the nature of the apprentice's contribution to the work.

In a sense, the artists of our time such as Christo, have solved the problem of identity by limiting the collaboration of other specialized crafts, a sort of adapted neo-Middle Age style. The chief designer (*Maître d'œuvre*) and the studio supervisor have given way to an artist who invents a unique form of expression: the megalomaniac of modern art. The apprentice has no place within this context, where Christo starts and finishes with Christo. Now the craftsperson takes the place of the apprentice, and the personal interpretation is eliminated.

Although for the art teacher the situation is quite different, there remain certain parallels with the art world that can help to guide art educators. The type of pedagogy that is required for collective works relates simultaneously to teaching, animating, effective distribution of the tasks, and management of diverse contributions by students at each stage of the project. This realisation enables teachers to acknowledge that the structure of a collective work is much richer and more flexible than it would appear at first glance.

## Goals of Collective Projects

Collective works correspond more to overall personal growth of the individuals than to the needs of a specific discipline. They aim to provide vigor and vitality to school life and its activities. These projects are often centered around annual cyclic events organized to correspond to seasons, cultural celebrations, and carnivals. The collaboration involved in such projects is usually based on the composition and spatial organization of one public display. Typically, it is assumed that the students already possess at least some of the technical knowledge required to participate.

There are three types of collective projects, the fruition of which will be determined by the desired type of composition, as well as the accessibility of materials.

The first and simplest kind of collective work is *accumulation*. The second is *collective gathering*, and the final is *collective hierarchization*.

## 1. Collective Projects of Accumulation

This type of project begins with the individual involvement of each participant, and it is a technique with which primary school teachers are already very familiar. A good example are autumn leaves or paper snowflakes which the pupils paste to a wall or a large piece of paper. Indeed, there exist many such forms of collective cut-up paper projects. Another example is the forest which is composed of shredded paper, and then glued and affixed together. Over time, the participants *inevitably discover overlapping*.

## 2. Collective Projects of Gathering and Distribution

This type of collectivity stems directly from the preceding example. The preoccupation here is a spatial one. Where and how does one place the trees so as to create the illusion of a forest, and to give the perception of depth? This also evokes such thematic projects as "The Farm" or "The Skating Rink." The various elements of these need to be distributed in such a way as to create a coherence to the image or the illusion of depth. This order is important since it allows the passage from schematic representation, which resembles the arrangement of a text, to the design of the composition which implies a particular point of view, meaningful overlap and superimposition. We can imagine themes such as "Born sixteen years ago" or "Family Portraits" in which the arrangement of the elements or the details of the composition become very important.

## 3. Collective Projects of Distribution and Hierarchization

This is the most complex form of collective project. The problem here is the need for selection and hierarchizing of the elements provided by all contributors. It is the type of project in which secondary school art teachers are challenged when they must, for example, mount a mural or an installation at the school entrance. If we think of a scene such as a "nativity," one must choose which characters, which characteristics need to be represented, how to prioritize them in terms of the spatial composition, and who or what to exclude. This kind of project also raises the problem of balance, or harmony of the image. How does one work colours together in a school mural?

The world of art provides many answers to this question and it is once again Rubens who offers the best lesson in this regard. For example, *Adam and Eve* in Lahaye has the characters painted by Rubens, the plant life by Jean Breughel, and the rabbits scurrying through the undergrowth by Franz Sneiders. The *Vision of St. Anthony* in Madrid, and *Achilles' Feast* in New York, offer two good examples of paintings done jointly by Rubens and Jean Breughel. Rubens would also have had the collaboration of Lucas Van Uden for *Diane and Calisto*. In *Diane and the Nymphs*, the countryside and the animals are attributed to Jean Wildens. In *The Adoration of the Magi* in Brussels, Rubens bestowed upon Van Dyck the task of linking together the figures and the stairway. Without doubt, history of art abounds with examples of exchanging skills in the realisation of a painting.

## The Problem of Harmonizing a Collective Image

We can reflect here on how to conceive of, in advance, the harmonization of shapes and colours within the collective image. In a complex collective project such as a Hierarchized Collective Project, harmonization depends upon the instructions given by the person who is overseeing its realisation. These need to be sufficiently laconic so as to allow the group to solve the problem themselves. Could we therefore say then, that the teacher must not intervene? On the contrary, we believe that she or he must intervene right from the beginning. The broad instructions come from the teacher; however, eventually they fade and serve only as reminders of the original concept. In addition, when there are overlapping images to be coordinated, one must never lose sight of the final product. Can one participant hide the contribution of another? We believe that, yes, she or he can, insofar as the overlap is partial and makes a positive contribution to the total picture.

It is here that visual language acquires its social value since it becomes the *lingua franca* for all the members of the group. Thus the intervention of the teacher becomes essential since she or he must stimulate the group's development in such a way as to avoid the outcome of the lowest common denominator.

## The Problem of Leadership

For us, collectivity in the art class does not come from a chosen pedagogical model. To be truly effective, a collective experience in the art class must draw its support from an external order, which becomes transformed into a tangible result, that being the group spirit. Thus, students in the school context feel like they belong to a community. This is what creates school spirit.

According to Cohen (1994), group work should be defined as a situation in which students work together in groups which are sufficiently small so that individuals participate fully in the task assigned to them. More specifically, the art teacher often deals with large groups, dividing them off into appropriate subgroups corresponding to specific tasks: Each group is responsible for solving a specific problem in a collective image: Which kinds of vegetation work best? What sorts of vehicles should be included? Which types of birds? Which types of characters? This provides a favorable framework to develop cooperative attitude between the students who share a common goal, a collective image to be achieved, under the guidelines stated by the teacher. There is effectively only one question related to leadership that arises here and it is linked to the question of status. Visual/haptic types, (visual equivalent of rational/emotional personalities) as defined by Lowenfeld (1947) can guide the art teacher even if the students are unaware of them. In the art class, the division of tasks can be executed in several ways: "I draw well, while you have a good sense of colour," or "I am very familiar with and you really like fashion and the costumes."

Abilities can be equally divided according to the level of skill in drawing, colouring, contrasting, composition, or cognitive knowledge (how to draw a particular kind of bird). Some students will prepare the colours, others the surface, and yet others will hand out the materials. But abilities can also be shared at the level of composition: out of overlapping is born the real; out of regrouping is born the relief. Artistic notions appear as a natural consequence of the collective process.

When a student works independently, there are few restrictions in terms of the composition. The student creates directly on his or her paper and will change his or her representational and compositional strategies during the course of the work, as the image develops. In collective projects, the student is brought to realize the rules or limits of creating the pictorialness. And in the case of collective projects, the teacher is actually a contractor, with the subcontracting being left to the students. The proposed project or contract must be sufficiently open in order for the students to be motivated, and yet sufficiently limited to allow them to actually complete something tangible and visually interesting. Since individual contributions are crucial to team success, participants feel more involved (Abrami, Chambers, Poulsen, De Simone, d'Appolonia, & Howden, 1996).

In conclusion, this article demonstrates that collective projects can provide an opportunity for a worthwhile return to the way that artists over the ages have lived their experiences. When Rubens has a tapestry created from one of his sketches, *The Triumph of the Euchariste over Ignorance and Blindness* (Prado), there is a certain kinship with some contemporary projects such as *Le Pont-Neuf Empaquete* (wrapped-up) by Christo, which required the gathering of 300 specialized workers and 600 monitors divided into groups of 40 people.

The idea of collective works in the classroom or otherwise is interesting because the images produced are done by a group of students. The traditional concept of the authenticity of an image thus finds itself recontextualized.

## References

Abrami, P. C., Chambers, B., Poulsen, C., De Simone, C., d'Appolonia, S., & Howden, J. (1996). *L'Apprentissage coopératif: Théories, méthodes, activités.* Montréal: Éditions de la Chenelière. Montréal.

Cohen, E. G. (1994). *Le travail de groupe.* Montréal: Éditions Chenelières.

Erlande-Brandenburg, A., Pernoud, R., Gimpel, J., & Bechman, R. (1986). *Carnet de villard de hon-necourt.* Paris: Stock.

Hicks, L. H. (1994). Social reconstruction and community. *Studies in Art Education, 35*(3), 149-156.

Lowenfeld, V. (1947). *Creative and mental growth.* New York. Macmillan.

Vasari, G. (1983). Chapter 22. In A. Chastel (Ed.), *La vie des meilleurs peintres et sculpteurs et architecte* (pp. 281-296). Paris: Berger-Levraut.

# Art Education Wrapped/Trapped in Fun: The Hope and Plight of Recreation Centre Art Instructors

Lara M. Lackey
*University of British Columbia*

## Introduction

Although visual art is taught and learned within many social arrangements, art educators have tended to privilege the contexts of schooling (Degge, 1987). Art educational efforts sponsored by non-school based groups have sometimes been dismissed as educationally irrelevant, lacking in rigour, or viewed as competition that could further erode the place of art as a school subject. Certainly valid concerns have been raised about the serious implications of not providing art education in public school (Bourdieu, 1979/1984) or leaving it to artists who have not considered the complexities and political nature of art education practice (Chapman, 1992). We are as often guilty, however, of taking the constraints and harmful effects of school institutions for granted (May, 1994; Apple, 1990) and frequently allow them to go unchallenged. Maintaining a narrow focus on schooling has meant that we consistently exclude non-school realms from the art education conversation and limit the imagined possibilities of our profession in terms of the populations and relations of time, space, and power within public schools.

In addition, the inclination to equate "education" with schooling has diverted our attention away from alternative educational settings as sites for research. An anthology such as this one helps to foster a reconceptualization of the parameters of our field, one that embraces a broader notion of what counts as art education. The forming of "partnerships" and the hope for a stronger field overall that the term implies, however, may well be obstructed by misunderstanding non-school realms as institutional and educational environments. Through lack of recognition and acknowledgment, we may also tacitly undervalue teachers and learners whose work and experience of art education occurs outside schools. Where this is the case, we inadvertently undermine our own field.

The purpose of this paper, therefore, is to take seriously the experiences and workplace environments of a particular group of non-school art educators who work in community recreation centres. I explore recreation centres as contexts for art education by examining some of the motivations for and contextual realities of this work. Overall, I offer a construction of recreational art education that contradicts certain prevalent assumptions about the nature of this practice.

## Background

This paper draws on qualitative research which examines two community centres as material and ideological environments for art education and art experience (Lackey, 1997). From that study one set of data, acquired through interviews with 10 full-time staff members (three male and seven female community recreation centre programmers or administrators) and nine female instructors of short term (6-10 week) visual art/craft programs, is emphasized. I also rely on data selections from parent interviews, centre documents, and field notes.

The study was conducted within a municipal Parks and Recreation Department which oversees 21 community centres and 70 parks on the Canadian Pacific Coast. In one sense each centre is unique and must respond to neighbouring communities distinguished by socioeconomics and culture. Typically, however, centres are surrounded by parks and playing fields. In addition they house a gymnasium and include a selection of other facilities such as hockey rinks, racquetball courts, fitness centres, tennis courts, swimming pools, snack bars, pottery rooms, multipurpose rooms, and "games" rooms for pool, table tennis and video games.

Programming is offered for all age groups and comprises a vast and eclectic smorgasbord of topics: Orff music, karate, gardening, fitness classes, drawing, tole painting, dance, volleyball, computer classes, school-holiday child care, indoor skateboarding, preschool socialization and play classes, dog obedience, and so on. Reflecting historic roots in physical education and sport, the ambiance and culture of athletics and fitness continue to pervade the centres and facilities are heavily used by amateur organized sport organizations for children and adults. The centres are also meeting places for a variety of other community groups and clubs, however, and serve as sites for a diverse program of community events. Taken as a group, the centres make literally thousands of recreational programs and experiences available to residents of the municipality over the course of each year.

In this particular setting, a new arts policy has recently mandated an increase in public arts programming sponsored by the municipality, thereby forcing the question of how art and art education can and should merge with the realm of recreation.

I begin my discussion with a consideration of why people may choose or find themselves in recreation centre employment. I address some prevalent perspectives about the nature of leisure and how art programming is commonly understood to fit within recreational settings. I then list some of the contextual circumstances which tend not to be accounted for by these dominant claims, thereby complicating the everyday work experiences of community centre art instructors.

## Choosing Recreation

Some might assume that people who teach art in community centres do so because they are under-educated in relation to school-based teachers and can therefore find no better employment. Like Degge (1987), I did not find this to be the case. Rather, with one exception, the instructors with whom I spoke had all completed a degree in fine arts or education; the one remaining had completed a partial degree.

In part, explanations given about career decisions depended on whether instructors defined themselves more as artists or teachers, though the roles could not be clearly distinguished. Although all choices were fundamentally pragmatic and economic, instructors' talk revealed a range of complex motivations and life situations that led them to seek work as art teachers in community centres. Certainly for some, this teaching was partly a means to an end: gaining access to facilities or acquiring a supplemental income for work less draining than teaching advanced students (and which therefore allowed one to reserve energy for making art) were two such purposes. For others, although certified to teach in schools elsewhere, the time and expense of re-certification was prohibitive. One individual could not find full time work as an elementary art specialist. All of the instructors with whom I spoke enjoyed their teaching, believed it to be making an important contribution on a number of levels, and took their practice seriously, struggling with its complexities and working hard to provide meaningful and satisfying experiences for their students.

Although those with or planning to acquire education degrees were attracted to full time employment in the school system, they could nevertheless see advantages to teaching in recreation centres, and some also had misgivings about schools as contexts for learning about art:

> ...before I...taught in community centres,...I called a few people in the Board of Education with proposals. And their feedback was, it needs to be structured, it needs to be more history and/or techniques oriented, it needs to be all of these things. And I didn't feel that's what I wanted to do. It's funny, ironic, since I'm about to do [the teacher education program], so I may end up not teaching in schools. I'm hoping to bring some of what I feel they *need* [laughs], which is [some of the things] that I've been able to do in community centres. [art instructor]

In terms of institutional roles, instructors tended to understand art education practice in recreation centres as falling somewhere between the work of schools and a relatively expensive and socially prestigious children's art program sponsored by a local nonprofit society. Within this relationship, recreation centres were often viewed as both less authoritarian and judgemental than schools, and more democratically accessible than the nonprofit program.

This tendency to frame recreation centre work in relation to schools and other relevant institutions is replicated in the talk of centre program staff, who regularly viewed their own career decisions as involving a value judgment about work in recreation or schools.

> I went through, probably two years of Phys. Ed. and I realized I really didn't want to be in a school setting...I realized...that I really didn't want to be in a setting where people were forced to take something that I thought was fun. And so I started taking more recreation courses as options...And that's when I thought recreation is more where I want to be. [centre programmer]

Admittedly, some of these remarks reveal rather romanticized notions about art learning. In addition, they tend to assume a dualistic relationship between the institutions of schooling and recreation. Woven into these comments, however, are also assumptions that recreation centres can be construed as sites for alternative forms of learning. They indicate as well a yearning for a place where everyone can have equal access to art and leisure experience, and suggest the good and sincere intentions that these community centre workers and art teachers have. Simultaneously this talk is interesting in the way in which it merges with dominant perspectives in leisure studies.

Stokowski (1994, pp. 3-5), for example, provides an overview of prevalent leisure definitions within leisure studies literature and suggests that there has been a "clustering of traditional definitions [of leisure] around three main topics." These include a "feeling or attitude of freedom and release from constraint;" "leisure as a [self-determined] activity primarily chosen for its own sake;" and leisure as "non-obligated or discretionary time left over after the necessary commitments of work, family, and personal maintenance are met."

Underlying these definitions is also the expectation that recreation should be pleasurable and fun. This assumption is applied equally to art programming in the centres and can be discovered in staff talk as well as in course descriptions:

> ...So I guess when I look at our programs I hope that when somebody comes out they'll be happy and if they're happy I feel that means that they felt comfortable expressing themselves in the program. [So my hope is that the program can break down any barriers to that comfort. [excerpt from an interview with a centre programmer]

### Oil Painting (Adults)

Learn basic oil painting techniques or further develop your own skills in this fun class. Learn basic colour theory and some drawing techniques.

Demos and lots of personal attention. All painting levels welcome. [document excerpt, course description]

Together these claims about leisure as a realm of freedom, pleasure, non-obligation, self-direction, and as generally lacking in coercion or frustration create a distinct ideological framework for art education in community centre settings, and delineate a practice that one research participant referred to as "not recreation, but education wrapped in fun."

The difficulty for instructors, however, lies in the fact that while these modernist claims form expectations for their work, they also obscure a number of social and contextual realities with which recreational art teachers must grapple. In this vein, I have come to view art education in recreation as not only "wrapped" in but simultaneously "entrapped" and restricted by notions of pleasure and fun in certain ways.

## Pleasure, Freedom, And Commodity

Claims that leisure occurs out of free choice and the need for instructors to ensure participants' pleasure are both related to the reality that these courses are also commodified leisure "packages" and students are clients. In this sense, course descriptions are written to appeal to the largest possible audience and to entice the purchase of the product. Art learning and education in this framework are commonly represented as enjoyable and soothingly therapeutic leisure experience. In keeping with what Mercer (1986) writes about ways that popular newspapers interweave pleasure and information, the descriptions create a "tissue of confirmations, beliefs, and expectations" (p. 55) about both the nature of artistic processes and the experience to be anticipated in the centre.

Clark and Critcher (1985) discuss how commercialism in leisure is often obscured by posing it as "the framework of opportunity within which individuals make choices in attempting to satisfy their leisure needs" (p. 100). They argue as well that such choice is not actually "free," but subject to social and economic constraints that include access to time, money and the capacity to imagine oneself comfortably participating in a given activity.

Gaining enough enrollment for courses is quite simply essential for community centre instructors, whose employment is literally lost without a specified minimum number of registrants. As such, ensuring that participants are pleased and satisfied tends to permeate this work and becomes an integral part of its everyday practice. Parents, for example, may make decisions about whether to re-enroll children in programs based on a perception of whether or not a child is having fun. As a result, instructors who ignore the call for fun may find themselves unemployed due to low enrollment in their courses. Parents can therefore use the threat of withdrawal as a kind of leverage through which program content is influenced.

Well, I was talking to [a dance instructor] saying, you know, unfortunately you're going to lose some of the kids. Callie [the speaker's daughter] has done it [taken class] the whole year, but a lot of them [the other children]-a third or half-just did the first session and quit. And…that was where I thought, it's just too much serious stuff, and stretching. I'm sure it's really important, especially when you're my age, but at their age, five minutes of running around, they're limbered up enough. And it's probably very good. I can see they're developing good habits, but I would say, save that for the advanced class…When you have to start dragging kids to it and their reason is 'cause it's boring, you're going to defeat yourself. She can run it that way, she's just not going to have a whole lot of kids continuing on, because most parents don't put up with dragging their kids to things. I mean, if they're not wanting to do it more than two or three times in a row, you're going, okay, next time we won't do this. [interview excerpt, parent]

## Fragmentation and Frenzy

The pleasurable sense of freedom in time, space, and mental state that is suggested by dominant leisure philosophy is complicated as well by the highly fragmented nature of recreation classes and the reality that these experiences occur within the context of an often frenzied modern world. Rojek (1993) notes the ways in which we have grown to accept leisure that is "partial and episodic" (p. 44) rather than deeply engaging, and likens dominant forms of leisure provided by media, film, and sport to "distraction factories" (Rojek, 1995, p. 11). In a similar way, recreation centres can sometimes be accused of creating distracted, agitated, and broken experience rather than that which is focused or even "leisurely."

Rarely, for example, do these classes occur in a time frame that is open, ongoing, and fluid, but more commonly take place in brief rigid blocks with clearly specified starts and ends, after which the program, and the relationship of students and teacher, abruptly disappear. Instructors experience the effects of this fragmentation when they must travel from site to site to teach, dealing with continually changing students, settings, and "bosses" over the course of each week and each short-term session.

Students, on the other hand, fit these courses into busy lives. Children, particularly those whose parents are more affluent or who use leisure programs as child care, may experience "leisure" as an unrelenting stream of programmed activity.

My idea is to expose them to a lot of things, and not necessarily get them doing any one thing, so they do skating [at one community centre]; gymnastics [at the university program]; and…Callie was doing jazz dance here…We do badminton…The clay class that Jason was in, he did that because Callie was doing jazz dance and so what could he do-and it's kinda fun anyway-and he was having so much fun at it, Callie now does jazz dance, and then there's a bit of overlap, Jason hangs around 'till Callie can get down, and then Callie does [clay class too]. Callie, because she really likes it. And we're really busy. Just in terms of, if anything, we don't have enough days when we do nothing, which we're sort of trying to [change]...She's in baseball right now, which is great, but it's horrible on the schedule...for the whole household...It's a short season, which is good, but it's erratic. Callie had five games in seven days. [Interview excerpt, parent]

## Lack of Authority

While art educators working in schools are imbued with a level of authority that weights their words and actions (Bourdieu & Passeron, 1977/1990), recreation centre instructors arguably work with the formal *lack* of authority associated with recreation centres as institutions of play (and not work). Art instructors may experience this as part of an ongoing struggle to engage students in meaningful activity. As one of them commented:

It's really frustrating teaching after school art because the kid's expectation is to not really have to do anything that counts. I mean, I had one kid who kept saying, "This doesn't really *count,* right? This doesn't really *count.*" And I think that they're so burnt out from school sometimes that they really...aren't ready to put a lot of thought in something.

The expectation that programs will be easy and fun combined with this official lack of power tend to complicate factors like children's behavior management as well as student motivation. But while all recreation workers must grapple with a general lack of status, the authority of art instructors is further undermined by the centre culture which privileges physical activity and sport.

## The Flexible Instructor

Within these kinds of recreational environments the "ideal" art instructor is often described by staff as "flexible." This can mean having a capacity to balance course formats in a style that is vaguely neither "too loose" nor "too structured," providing just enough of a format that the class appears organized, but is not so rigid that students cannot move in directions of their own interest. In this sense it can refer to a lack of insistence on your own agenda as instructor and a willingness to bend to student wishes. Certainly it suggests the need to continually attend to a state of student happiness.

Instructors, however, report feeling frustrated and demoralized when, after deliberately "un-structuring" their courses, they are then accused of being "too loose" in their teaching approaches or "not really teaching."

Being flexible can also mean being "accepting." This is accomplished on one hand by welcoming a range of student abilities in one's class, but on another it suggests resigning oneself to the often less than ideal conditions and levels of support that the community centre may provide for this work, and letting go of some of one's hopes for student accomplishment:

> Yeah. I think flexible is probably the word. Because…I don't want a teacher [to say], "Hey, go home and practice ten hours a day and then come back to the next session"…I think people are there and what you're trying to do is to expose them and educate them to…an appreciation. What ever it might be. And to introduce some skills. But at the same time, not to have these great expectations. [For example] if they don't fit, kick them out of the class…Sure, there's age appropriateness and there's other factors. But the ability thing, I don't think should be a factor. So I think you've got to be flexible with that. Take the good with the bad, the budding with the not so talented…[In addition] I think they [instructors] have to live with us [the centre]. I would warn them that [they may have to be satisfied with less expensive materials] and they're going to be educating our staff [because staff members are not usually knowledgeable about visual art materials]. And, so its just to be a little more flexible with staff, and educating them to what's available…And, yeah, there are all sorts of pains that are associated with someone [an instructor] who has got a really high standard. [interview excerpt, centre administrator]

## Conclusion

This discussion suggests several ways in which prevalent perceptions about the nature of art instruction in recreation institutions can be called into question. One example is the assumption that recreational art instructors are necessarily under-qualified and have few other employment options. Rather, the art instructors with whom I spoke chose their work for many reasons and had a broad range of education and experience. Further, although recreation centres are places where artists teach, they are also sites of practice for art educators who have been "pushed" from formal education by credentialing processes or lack of employment in a marginal field. Of those who might otherwise work in schools, some deliberately choose recreation out of a sense of hope that these settings might offer a positive and alternative form of art education to that which schools are perceived to provide. These ideas complicate assumptions that present these non-school practitioners as lacking in expertise or commitment. Rather, they suggest that the value distinctions often made between school and non-school art education practices may frequently result from arbitrary rules or grow from the same social conditions which influence the under-valuing of art in schools.

The tendency to dismiss recreation centre practice as irrelevant, easy work which is just for fun, or to romanticize it as a realm of freedom to which anyone can have access is also challenged in this paper. The image of practice that emerges is one in which instructors' hopes for a free and un-coerced environment for student learning may be undermined by the centres' inter-relationships with commercialism, the often extreme fragmentation that is imposed on programming, and the status and perceptions of the role of art teacher in an institution with an "officially" low status which continues to privilege the realm of physical education and athletics.

These points hold important implications for the formation of collaborative relationships or institutional partnerships in art education. One is that true collaboration seems unlikely if we do not first question presuppositions that stratify art education practice according to the context in which it occurs. We need to begin to understand, acknowledge, and support the work of people teaching art in non-school environments; we cannot sincerely collaborate as unequal partners.

Furthermore, contrary to assumptions embedded in the prevalent perspectives, recreation centres are complex institutions which hold both opportunities and contraints for art education practice, and therefore deserve and require careful examination if institutional partnerships are to be strengthened. Until we begin to analyze rather than dismiss the ways in which art education practices fit within such settings, we can understand neither the common ground on which partnerships might be built nor the work that needs still to be done in terms of standards that we can agree upon and expect. In turn, analyzing the ways in which art fits into recreation centres provides a means to compare and contrast the place of art in schools. We then have the opportunity to consider where unfounded boundaries between schools and recreation centres begin to dissolve, and to clarify the broader frameworks and circumstances that influence all art educational institutions.

# References

Apple, M. W. (1990). *Ideology and curriculum* (2nd ed.). New York: Routledge.

Bourdieu, P., & Passeron, J. C. (1977/1990). *Reproduction in education, society, and culture* (R. Nice, Trans.). London: Sage.

Bourdieu, P. (1979/1984). *Distinction: A social critique of the judgement of taste* (R. Nice, Trans.). Cambridge, MA: Harvard University Press.

Chapman, L. H. (1992). Arts education as a political issue: The federal legacy. In R. A. Smith & R. Berman (Eds.), *Public policy and the aesthetic interest: Critical essays on defining cultural and educational relations* (pp. 119-136). Urbana: University of Illinois Press.

Clark, J., & Critcher, C. (1985). *The devil makes work: Leisure in capitalist Britain.* Houndsmills, England: Macmillan.

Degge, R. M. (1987). A descriptive study of community art teachers with implications for teacher preparation and cultural policy. *Studies in Art Education, 28*(3), 164-175.

Lackey, L. (1997). *Pedagogies of leisure: Considering community recreation centres as contexts for art education and art experience.* Unpublished doctoral dissertation, University of British Columbia, Vancouver.

May, W. (1994). The tie that binds: Reconstructing ourselves in institutional contexts. *Studies in Art Education, 35*(3), 135-148.

Mercer, C. (1986). Complicit pleasures. In T. Bennet, C. Mercer, & J. Woollcott (Eds.), *Popular culture and social relations* (pp. 50-68). Philadelphia: Open University Press.

Rojek, C. (1993). *Ways of escape: Modern transformation in leisure and travel.* Houndsmills, England: Macmillan.

Rojek, C. (1995). *Decentring leisure: Rethinking leisure theory.* London: Sage.

Stokowski, P. A. (1994). *Leisure in society: A network cultural perspective.* New York: Mansell.

## Part II

# Voices Within Communities

## Moving the Mountain: Linking Higher Art Education and Communities

Fiona Dean

*Glasgow School of Art*

*As communities embark on processes of renewal, the challenge for art education is to locate itself within the changing societal framework, creating a process for learning and exchange between the institution and wider society.*

A critical analysis and evaluation of art objects has always played a significant and important part in the education of artists. However, as the role, function and place of the artist in society changes and develops, so too do the challenges for tertiary art education. Many local and international models offer examples of community partnerships in education and the arts that establish processes for participation. Most importantly, these models also demonstrate ways in which higher education can actively seek and forge links with community-based initiatives, establishing a two-way process for learning and exchange between the institution and the community.

Why are these issues important to explore? Many of our communities reflect the characteristics of years of neglect. Severe social and economic deprivation is characterized by a range of factors: poor housing, environments, high unemployment and low educational achievement. In many inner city and peripheral housing schemes, young people are growing up amidst the realities of second- and third-generation unemployment, often leading to low expectations, low self-esteem and a fear of failure that prevents participation.

Amongst many other things, the recent Kennedy report (1997) advocates for education to be extended from traditional learning centers and delivered in a diversity of other, more accessible contexts. It also underlines that in the UK, only 1% of higher education students are likely to come from the socially and economically disadvantaged backgrounds all too prevalent in many communities within our cities (Kennedy, 1997). There are strong moral, social, and ethical needs to address this gap of opportunity. Perhaps also, it is a misunderstanding of the realities many communities face: their needs as well as the many successful ways in which they themselves are tackling such serious issues.

In considering the future of our cities and communities there are of course conflicting schools of thought. Some suggest that the way forward is to "depopulate" these "places with many vices and few if anything of merit," and bring "their long suffering inhabitants back to the real city where they belong" (Stamp, 1997, p. 19). Far from having nothing of merit, there are many things that could and should be looked to and learned from in considering plans for the future.

## Drawing On Local Experience

Easterhouse, the largest of Glasgow's peripheral housing schemes, has a population of 37,000 people. More than 40% of the population are under the age of 25 and almost half of the working-age population are unemployed.

Located at the center of the Lochend community is the Easterhouse Mosaic. Covering a wall space of some 1500 sq. ft., the work is amongst one of the biggest of its kind in Europe. Even now, more than 13 years after its making, the Easterhouse Mosaic still offers a significant model for participation in the arts, community partnerships and renewal. In an area where lack of opportunity and resources often gives rise to high incidents of crime and vandalism, this ambitious work is still resplendent and free from damage or graffiti (see Figures 1-2).

The Community Housing Movement is yet another influential and inspiring model. Built on the principle of local control, there are approximately 50 community ownership groups all over Scotland that offer processes for participation and partnership. In addition to the physical transformation of damp and poor quality housing, a commitment to embedding jobs, training, and education within the infrastructure of the community is at the heart of most developments.

Figures 1 and 2. Easterhouse mosaic. Detail.

Community renewal and development offers challenges to implement new and sustainable approaches for the future. There are opportunities to build from the inside out, creating partnerships and sharing resources. Critically, what is missing from the picture is the practical link with higher education, not only in the arts but across a range of areas. Considered within this developing process, the potential role and function of art education can be explored as part of the strategic planning of communities.

Renewal also offers opportunity to explore issues of self, identity and culture. Over the course of 6 months, as part of the development of one community space, 12-18 year olds living in the Easterhouse area, most with no previous art experience, embarked on a process of exploration and discovery of these issues. By means of a partnership program between a community housing organization, the arts and education, individuals worked through the visual arts to develop personal ideas of self and sense of place.

The resulting images were both strong and powerful. First, the physicality and intimacy of self in relation to site and place was rendered through life-size photograms; self was then transposed and transformed through the acquisition of new skills and access to new technology; finally, self was viewed and represented as part of the wider community.

Many of these ideas were incorporated into the developing site and all participants gained accreditation from a local community college for their participation. For many young people it was not only their first experience in the arts, but their first encounter with the possibilities of further education and what that might entail and mean to them (Pocket Park, 1996).

## International Models

Beyond the magnificent architectural exterior of the city of Chicago, you are invited to move inwards to a "city of neighbourhoods," a city made up of culturally diverse communities. Pilsen is one such community. Predominantly Latino, mostly Mexican American, visual expression and architectural embellishment in the form of murals and signage, signal a strong sense of cultural identity.

Proposals for new housing in the community brought about a partnership between The University of Illinois at Chicago (UIC), Universidad Autonoma Metropolitana at Azcapotzalco (UAM), and the residents of Pilsen. Entitled "Housing, Community and Culture," it was a project that brought cultural and institutional exchange directly into the Pilsen community. The success of the partnership was such that it resulted in a request from the people of Pilsen for the consideration of a new collaboration, targeting the renewal of the 18th Commercial Street.

An important historic and economic center to the area, this project paved the way for further cross-cultural experience and partnerships. By working and interacting directly with the community, a link was created for learning and exchange between the institution and the community itself. Each responding to the needs and aspirations of the other and working towards the understanding and reinforcement of cultural expression.

However, cultural diversity does not always go hand in hand with cultural integration. Many of Chicago's neighbourhoods, such as Cabrini Green and Stateway Park reflect the arising sense of cultural and economic polarization. Within Stateway Park, a partnership amongst community, artists, educators and environmentalists is attempting to tackle these issues, with vacant lots of land being reclaimed and renewed in the form of community gardens. It is a transformation that is both practical and imaginative, providing food as well as a vehicle for creative reflection on the cultural iconography of the community (see Figure 3).

Both gardens are sited around one of Chicago's many youth centers. This particular center is home to Street Level Video's innovative media arts training program, which offers practical and creative opportunity to young people living in the area. Increasing numbers of university outreach and settlement programs are also establishing partnerships between locally based projects such as housing, youth and the arts, as a means of sharing institutional resources with communities.

The Department of Continuing Education at the School of the Art Institute of Chicago operates three, long-term art and education projects within areas of need

Figure 3. Stateway Park Community Garden. Detail.

throughout the city. Through links with further education colleges, many universities here at home have enabled further access to higher educational opportunity. Partnerships with locally based initiatives, carve pathways to further learning opportunity deep within the community and offer the potential to develop new and innovative models for access and participation.

Moving from Chicago to Minneapolis, the Phillips Gateway Project is one of a series of public art works organized by the Minneapolis Arts Commission. The proposal at Peavey Park differs from many others in that it offered various levels of community participation in the realisation of the work. Situated in the Phillips neighbourhood, the area is home to a mix of nearly every racial and ethnic community in Minnesota, including one of the largest urban Native American populations in the USA.

While the effects of neglect and its consequences can be seen in many aspects of the Phillips community, the creation of a small park offered opportunity for collaboration, education, and training through the arts for hundreds of young people in area. Projects in and out of school again explored cultural imagery and iconography, which was transferred into the physical elements of the work (see Figure 4). Moreover, beyond the creation of a valuable and necessary new amenity, this and other art related projects also established important links between community organizations and higher education.

Figure 4. Phillips Gateway project. Detail.

The Higher Education Consortium for Urban Affairs (HECUA) each year places students within a diversity of arts organizations throughout the city of Minneapolis. Students of participating universities from all over Minnesota, can apply to undertake a semester of study at the Minneapolis-based City Arts Program. These are students from a mix of specializations, not only the visual arts, who come together to study and contribute practically to working arts organizations.

In addition to the experience of placement, the program encourages critical and analytical debate as to the role and function of the arts within the process of community development. In doing so, students in turn question their own developing practice in relation to issues facing communities, seeing the application and shaping of their practice in other contexts.

There is a need to recognize, explore and learn from cultural and communal interaction. In Mexico, the sense of cultural dichotomy is overwhelming. Here the dynamics of the city sit hand-in-hand with the timelessness of ancient sites; contemporary art re-presents modern self and the other; ritual and revolution exist side by side. Amidst these rich and stark contrasts, the "Colorín Colorado" project was established. Developed by the Trust for the Health of Indian Children of Mexico (Colorín Colorado: The Art of Indian Children, 1994), one of the central aims of the organization is to bring equality and parity to some of the most remote, marginalized, and yet culturally rich and complex communities from all over Mexico.

Part of the process of establishing equality is recognizing the wealth and importance of cultural identity. "Colorín Colorado" is a series of large-scale canvases, painted collaboratively by children from 17 of the country's culturally diverse indigenous groups. These massive murals depict traditions, customs, rituals and stories form day-to-day life. Almost every available space on the huge canvases is packed with detail, narrative and an explosion of color. But perhaps one of the most striking elements of the imagery, is the portrayal of self as part of the collective. Each individual is seen as a functioning and necessary part of the whole community.

Our teleological society has a great deal to look to and learn from other communities, and we ignore the existing culture and identity of people and places at the greatest of costs. The project established a labyrinth of partnerships, and offers a means to both celebrate and learn from communities where art and culture seem inextricably bound together.

In New York City, The Public Art Development Fund recently financed two artists to work in the same Lower East Side community. Sited at the Williamsburg bridge, artist Chris Doyle's piece was an attempt to reinstate the sense of passage from one side of the bridge to the other. The resulting gilding of the stairway not only altered space physically, but symbolically referred to the transition from poverty to a better way of life offered at the other side of the river. A poetic idea, but one whose poetry was consumed by the prevalent street culture, even the information sign was wiped out by the voracity of the graffiti.

A few blocks away, the undeniably energetic imagery of mostly illicit paintings, emblazon walls, vans and anything that remains static for too long (see Figure 5). Amidst this Brett Cook-Dizney offers a series of portraits of young people attending school in the area. Painted directly on to the school wall, this massive painting, "See What We See," is a powerful blend of image and text. "I go to school," "I learn to represent." Dizney's recognition of both context and constituency—the users of the space and their sense of ownership—is reflected in his chosen methodology, content and approach. Painted with the spray can, a familiar tool within the area, the portraits are a strong, poetic, and sophisticated statement on the importance and dignity of self and identity.

## The Challenges For Art Education

Higher art education has tremendous potential to re-envision itself within a partnership process that responds to the widening roles and functions of the artist as both facilitator and enabler. Fine art practice and education, with the depth and breadth of their diagnostic base, are ideally placed to meet these challenges, equip-

Figure 5. "Live by the gun, die by the gun." Street Mural.

ping artists with the diversity of skills necessary to operate in a range of contexts. The individual operates as part of a collective.

Reflecting on many of these issues, in her book "Zones of Contention," Becker (1996), Dean of Visual Arts at the School of the Art Institute of Chicago, describes how in her view, "the art world has become increasingly hermetic, its discourse often incomprehensible to those outwith its closed system" (p. 87).

In an attempt to address some of these issues, a conference took place between students and faculty from the School of the Art Institute of Chicago, San Francisco Art Institute and the Corcoran School of Art and Design, Washington, DC. The focus of the "Artists As Citizens" symposium at the Headlands Center, Sausalito, was to debate and explore "how" and "why" art institutions might evolve in response to a changing society. During such financially competitive and difficult times for institutions, particularly the arts and education, this was a unique gathering and forum for the sharing of ideas.

As Becker (1977) describes, the debate revolved around a number of topics, such as century-old mission statements that preceded significant and influential movements in the arts, technological advances, cultural and societal change. It discussed the increasing number of graduates and artists who are choosing to operate in a diversity of fields outside the gallery-dominated art world and what implications this might have for teaching and learning strategies. Most importantly, it underlined that the future must mean more than the establishment of new courses. "Perhaps the greatest transgression" writes Becker (1997) is "in owning them institutionally" (p. 14).

At the center of such debate lies a series of questions with which so many artists and educators struggle and equally as many choose to ignore: what is the importance of creativity without the confines of the art world and what is the function and value of art and its wider application in society? The Headlands Conference gave students an opportunity to prepare and present their views and desires in relation to this: the need for more practical skills in the business of administration and negotiation; greater understanding of the history of the artist's place in society; their very real concern to operate as artists, activists, and educators in communities (Becker, 1997).

The curriculum must change and adapt to reflect and cultivate these ambitions. At the School of the Art Institute of Chicago curriculum change resulted, with the introduction of a new undergraduate elective, "The Art of Crossing the Street: Creativity and Community in the Twenty-First Century." A course to prepare art students to take greater initiative in allying and questioning their changing practice at the end of the 20th century (School of the Art Institute of Chicago, 1997).

At Glasgow School of Art, for the last 8 years a unique student-artist placement program has been operated by the Department of Historical and Critical Studies. This year alone it placed 70 students in schools and a diversity of educational settings, not as student *teachers*, but as student *artists*, learning through sharing their practice with others. This provides an important opportunity for experiential learn-ing and direct interaction with a range of situations, groups, and individuals throughout the city.

For many students, the challenge of taking part lies not only with the negotia-tions involved in setting up the placement and their planned program, but the real-ities they encounter: the needs of young people, staff, schools, organizations, com-munities. How ideas and practice operate within this and indeed are shaped by it, is fundamental to the learning experience. The shaping of practice is not only through context as so many courses now address, but through constituency—prac-tice mediated through people and their needs.

Such programs offer the potential for artists and students to see themselves as part of the collective potential of a community. They ally the methodologies of art practice, the highly reflexive, inductive, deductive and critical processes that lie at the center of creativity, within the very action of community development.

Art practice and education can underpin the sense of ownership necessary to tackle the realities, needs and critical issues facing communities. In turn, through these connections and partnerships, art practice and education can be influenced by these realities. Tertiary art education and other areas of higher education have the potential to be actively and critically involved in this level of debate. A debate that should not be confined within the institution, but must surely look to, learn from and seek partnership with a wide range of successful community based initia-tives.

As communities embark on processes of renewal, the challenge for art education is to locate itself within the changing societal framework, creating a process for learning and exchange between the institution and wider society. The potential is there to apply the learning and understanding that grows from such collaborations, to the development of ideas for the future.

## References

Becker, C. (1996). *Zones of contention*. Albany: State University of New York Press.

Becker, C. (1997, March). Training citizen artists. Art and education conference report. *Artweek*, 13-14.

*Colorín Colorado: The art of Indian children*. (1994). Mexico: Trust for the Health of Indian Children.

Kennedy, H. Q. C. (1997). *Learning works widening participation in further education*. Coventry, UK: Further Education Funding Council.

Pocket Park Project, Art and Community Regeneration. (1996). Glasgow, UK. [Brochure].

School of the Art Institute of Chicago. (1997). *New course on creativity and community*. Program infor-mation for incoming students.

Stamp, G. (1997, April 27). Now is the time for Glasgow to rise again from the ruins of the worst laid schemes. *Scotland on Sunday*, p. 19.

# The Dinner Party

Philip J. Perry
*Monash University*

This paper describes a partnership in art project sponsored in Australia in 1994 by Monash University, the Mornington Peninsula Arts Centre and 15 primary schools from the Victorian State, Independent, and Catholic school systems. Over 700 children were involved in this undertaking.

About 18 years ago the visual arts were well served in primary schools across the state of Victoria, Australia. There was a qualified art specialist in every school with an enrollment of 225 or more. Many schools had purpose-built art rooms, built from funds raised by the local community and matched by the Department of Education. There was a group of 25 to 30 specialists, called the Primary Arts Branch, stationed in Melbourne, which gave inservice workshops across the state, helped with curriculum development, prepared support materials, and so on. Art advisers were stationed in each of the 51 inspectorial districts across the state. In charge of the Arts Branch was a senior administrator called the Supervisor of Art. (Perry, 1990).

The specialist art teachers were most often well-trained, having completed a one-year end-on Arts course. Others of these qualified specialists had undergone intensive short courses. Art flourished in schools, most specialists working closely with classroom teachers by using the art program, at least in part, to complement the class teaching program, and by encouraging an extension of the art program into the classroom. As may be surmised, the work produced by children who took such thoughtful, sequential programs, taught by such committed teachers, was of a very high standard indeed.

This wonderful state of the arts, however, has not survived. Over a short period of time State government policies, designed both to cut expenditure and to devolve much of the responsibility for programs and staffing to the schools themselves, have resulted in the structure outlined above crumbling away. There is now no central group of art educators at all, the Ministry of Education's policies having left the responsibility for catering for arts education to individual schools, sometimes with quite disastrous results. In fact, under the Ministry's "Schools of the Future" plan, it seems that it is possible for schools, at their own discretion, to select people with absolutely no teaching qualifications at all to teach their arts programs. This may well be a strategy suited to cutting expenditure, but "Schools of the Future" seems a strange title for such institutions.

Much has been written about who should teach art: readers are referred to the work of, for example, Lansing (1969), Dobbs (1986), Ball (1990) and Rabey (1994), and to the National Policies of the Australian Institute of Art Education (Perry, 1991). The general view is that, at primary level, there should be an art specialist working cooperatively with the generalist teachers within a school, in much the same fashion as earlier described. The problem is, of course, that for art educators in Victoria to argue this point is purposeless, since the structure that allowed such collaboration has been dismantled.

The situation in the Independent and Catholic school systems is somewhat different. Indeed, it appears from some fairly recent research (Deakin University, Monash University, University of Melbourne, & Cross Arts Victoria, 1994) that the arts are in a much healthier state in those systems.

To summarise thus far: In Victoria, Australia, there are signs that the arts, at least within the State system, are becoming increasingly marginalised.

It seemed to me that initial teacher training institutions should not stand aside as uninterested—nor even disinterested—observers. I believed that Monash University could play a part in trying to arrest this process. If Monash could encourage schools to participate in a large, well-publicised, cooperative project which would attract public attention, then the arts (within those schools which chose to participate) would assume greater importance. The project I chose was "The Peninsula Dinner Party." The idea was prompted by Judy Chicago's original *Dinner Party* and, also, by a children's version I had seen exhibited in Montreal, in 1993, as part of the World Congress of the International Society for Education through Art. The work had been completed by children from a number of Canadian schools and was exhibited in a large shopping mall for the duration of the conference.

Furthermore, I thought that the metaphor of "famine" (applied to primary school art in Victoria) counteracted by "feast," was attractive. And I hoped that our cooperative "menu" would sustain participants and nurture art in the schools.

I approached Elizabeth Gleeson, Director of the Mornington Peninsula Arts Centre, situated 15 kilometres from Monash, who greeted the idea with immediate enthusiasm. We decided to invite the participation of all primary (elementary) schools within the Mornington Peninsula Region and, to this purpose, we sent a letter, in October 1993, to the principals of all such schools. The letter explained what we hoped to achieve, hinted at the publicity that the school might gain, and invited participation. Of the 69 letters we sent, we received 15 "acceptances." Here is the letter:

Dear Principal,
We are writing to you on behalf of the Mornington Peninsula Arts Centre and the Faculty of Education at Monash University, Peninsula Campus.

What we hope to be able to arrange with you is the creation of a child art display to be exhibited at the Gallery during Education Week next year. The display will consist of a Dinner Party of papier mâché figures made by children from primary schools on the Mornington Peninsula. Each participating school would be responsible for one or two "settings" at the table (the actual number will depend upon how many schools are interested in taking part). A "setting" will consist of one seated figure, a chair, plates, dishes, cutlery, a place mat, a food dish and a table ornament. Everything would be made of papier mâché except the chair upon which each figure was seated. Everything would have to be made according to specifications which we will supply to participating schools.

The names of all participating students and schools will be displayed next to the exhibit and in any programs we produce. We will make every effort to have the event publicised in the media.

Would you please let us know whether your school is interested in taking part in the creation of "The Peninsula Dinner Party." Because we expect a good response we will restrict participation to those schools responding by Friday, 6 November. If we have too many entries by then, it will have to be "first in, best dressed," so please reply promptly if you are interested (over sixty schools have been sent this letter).

Yours sincerely,

| | |
|---|---|
| Elizabeth Gleeson | Dr. Phil Perry |
| Director | Faculty of Education |
| Mornington Peninsula Arts Centre | Monash University |

In November [1993] we sent the art teachers of those 15 schools a letter thanking them for their expressions of interest. The letter also detailed, in very specific terms, the dimensions of each figure to be submitted, and of each table setting (plates, cups, glasses, cutlery, and so on). Schools which indicated a wish to construct two figures were given details of their second figure: waitresses and waiters, a vocalist, and a guitarist.

By early May [1994] one of us (sometimes both) had managed to visit all 15 schools to take photographs of work in progress and to ensure that the project was keeping to schedule.

Schools involved in the project approached it in different ways, concentrating their efforts on the particular kinds of learning that fitted their individual policies and curricula. Three examples will help to explain this.

One non-government school used the project to introduce, and then reinforce, drawing and modelling skills in its year 6 students (all boys). It had two teachers pose for its figures—a woman dressed in a dinner gown, a waiter carrying a tray of

wine bottles and glasses. The art teacher took photographs of the two volunteers from several angles (front, back, profile, close-up) and these were used as guidelines for the children. The work of several artists, including Judy Chicago, was viewed and discussed. Methods of making the figures, place settings, clothing and so on, were decided in group discussions. Teams of about 18 boys were responsible for making each of the two models and their accoutrements.

The art learning that went on at this school was clearly concentrated on the techniques, skills, and understandings required to produce accurate representations. It was reinforced through example and discussion.

One large government school, on the other hand, had, as its main objective, the involvement of all of its year 4, 5 and 6 classes (over 150 students) in a cooperative endeavour. The aim was for these children to participate in a collaborative artmaking project and, by so doing, to experience and understand the nature of such collaborations. That this occurred through art was not as important as the fact that the children learned to work together to fulfill a common purpose, to achieve a common target.

With such large numbers, of course, more decisions, at least in the early stages of the project, were made by the teacher rather than by the students.

Another government school decided to allow only two classes to participate. About 16 boys and girls made each of the two figures that this school produced. Here, the aim was for the children to contribute creatively to the making of "their" models. The art teacher acted as a hard-working facilitator, rather than as a guide or director, the children themselves making their own decisions about methods to be employed, colours to be used, and articles to be made for place settings.

The really interesting thing about these different learning experiences was that they all produced positive results: children were enthused and excited. All were proud of "their" figure, whether they were part of a team of 10 or 75. One may deduce from this, I think, that it is the enthusiasm, commitment, and professionalism of the teacher that sparks the children's excitement in art, not necessarily the curriculum or its aims and objectives. The best advocate for art education is the enthusiastic art teacher.

By May most schools had finished or nearly finished their figures. Late that month we sent out a final letter which set out delivery instructions and details of the opening ceremony. All figures and settings were finished on time and delivered to the gallery. A catalogue was prepared which listed every school, every teacher and, most importantly, every child who had participated.

We invited groups, to a maximum of 8 people, from each school to the opening of the exhibition but, somehow or other, nearly 150 attended. The exhibition was opened by a Melbourne comedienne, Evelyn Krape, who arrived in the guise of "Felicity St. John Fairweather," famous art expert and adviser to the National Gallery of Melbourne (you can imagine the children's reaction to this apparition, who brought with her a dish of fish-heads on a base of hundreds-and-thousands).

## What were some of the tangible results of this experiment?

1. So many family and school groups booked to see the exhibition that it was kept on display for 2 months—double the time originally scheduled.

2. According to the Director, many families and children were introduced to the Gallery for the first time and have since returned to see other exhibitions.

3. The Australian Broadcasting Corporation made a short film of the exhibition which was shown on one of its Statewide current affairs programs.

4.Four local weekly newspapers publicised the children's work prominently—three on the front page.

5. *The Dinner Party* was reassembled and displayed in October 1994 at the Royal Exhibition Buildings as part of Melbourne's 4th Annual Contemporary Art Fair.

6. When the *Dinner Party* project was completed, all figures ended up in prominent display positions at their "home" schools, most in an entrance foyer.

What was the significance of the project? Clearly, it resulted in the value of art being confirmed and reinforced for all those schools and children who participated in the project, and for all the families involved, too. It has been followed by "The Peninsula Jazz Band," which attracted similar crowds. As well, a colleague—Jane Chia—has conducted a similar project in Singapore.

The project has now been handed over to my Monash University colleague, Ms. Geraldine Burke, who is enthusiastically developing cooperative links between district schools and her own Studio Arts students at Monash University. The future of this ongoing collaborative project looks very bright.

I firmly believe that cooperative schemes such as this could be readily organised by artists, art educators, universities, and the like. It seems to me that *everybody* benefited from the scheme—most importantly of all, the children who took part.

## References

Ball, L. (1990). What role: Artist or teacher? *Art Education, 43*(1), 54-59.

Deakin University, Monash University, University of Melbourne, Cross Arts Victoria. (1994). *Submission to the senate inquiry into arts education.* Melbourne: Author.

Dobbs, S. M. (1986). Generalists and specialists: Teaming for success. *Design for Arts in Education, 87*(6), 39-42.

Lansing, K. (1969). *Arts, artists and art education.* New York: McGraw Hill.

Perry, P. J. (1990). Salamanders, the Speewah, and the spirit's universe. *Australian Art Education, 14*(2), 87-91.

Perry, P. J. (Ed.). (1991). *National policies: The Australian Institute of Art Education.* Melbourne: Art Craft Teachers' Association.

Rabey, P. (1994). Who should teach art? In P. J. Perry (Ed.), *Readings in art education* (pp. 45-52). Melbourne: Monash University.

## Author's Note

This paper has been adapted from a presentation made to the Second InSEA-SEA-PAC Regional Congress held in Subic, the Philippines, in November 1994. I would like to thank all those who participated in the project.

# Art as a Way of Learning: A Business and Education Partnership

Patricia Pinciotti
*East Stroudsburg University*


Rebecca Gorton
*Northampton Community College*

The national school reform movement and educational research indicate that schools need to refocus teaching and learning to develop children's higher order thinking skills, address all types of learners and engage individuals in experiences which enhance understanding and personal meaning on a variety of levels (Fowler, 1996; The Goals 2000 Art Education Partnership, 1995). The centrality of the arts and its integration into the pedagogy of the schools can specifically address the challenges of the school reform movement.

Based on a 2-year study, business leaders have identified skills and competencies essential to the changing workforce (U.S. Department of Labor, 1991). They challenge educators, and in particular art educators, to add the integration of the arts into educational reform efforts. William H. Kolberg, President of the National Alliance of Business states that, "Today's global market and technological growth require every worker to solve problems, to work in teams, and to be creative" (Getty Center for Education in the Arts, 1993, p. 20). The arts provide a context for problem-posing and solving as students are given the opportunity to construct knowledge and demonstrate their understanding in meaningful ways.

Restructuring schools with the arts at the core requires teachers, arts specialists, administrators, and parents to critically examine the schools' teaching and assessment practices in the context of the challenges created by the school reform movement. Changing the way classroom teachers think, feel, and incorporate the arts in their teaching requires a paradigm shift. For children to live lives where the arts are central to their understandings and feelings, educators face a even deeper challenge. They must rethink the professional education of teachers. Systemic change with the arts as "basic" for teacher preparation and professional development requires a profound commitment on the part of teaching training institutions, basic education, business, and the arts community.

The purpose of this chapter is to examine a dynamic business and education partnership where the arts are at the core of the individual and shared goals, inherent in the process of collaboration and impact teacher education at an inservice and preservice level.

## The Partnership

Northampton Community College and Binney & Smith, Inc., both located in eastern Pennsylvania, responded to this challenge with a business and education partnership. The initial purpose of the partnership was to explore and develop multiple means to more fully and effectively infuse the arts into teaching and learning at the early childhood and elementary grade classrooms and teacher preparation programs.

Northampton Community College has a 2-year early childhood teacher preparation program which prepares graduates to teach young children birth to age 5, and /or to transfer to a 4-year teacher education institution. In 1991, Northampton Community College's faculty was preparing to reconceptualize their teacher preparation program to be consistent with emerging research and information related to teaching and learning, particularly with young children.

Binney & Smith, Inc., a manufacturer of artistic products, assumes an active advocacy role at the national, state, and local level helping art educators and arts agencies make a strong case for the value of the arts in the schools. Their involvement is motivated by a belief in the importance of the arts to everyday living. Richard S. Gurin, CEO of Binney & Smith, Inc., in an interview states,

> Arts education is the primary focus for our advocacy efforts because we believe that art fosters learning, creative and critical thinking, and self-expression from early childhood through adulthood. We believe the full range of arts disciplines should be part of the core curriculum in public education. We believe that stronger preparation in the arts will enable our children to cooperate and compete with the other nations of the world. (Pearson, 1993, p. 1)

Binney & Smith, Inc., a company with a vested interest in the arts, is a presence in the school reform movement and an advocate for the national arts standards. They recognize the importance of providing art specialists and classroom teachers with support for integrating the arts into daily teaching.

The initiatives of the two institutions shared a powerful common goal and joint commitment. Both groups wanted to make children's learning more meaningful and engaging, by strengthening the art educator's role in building collaborative relationships and providing classroom teachers with knowledge, basic skills, and dispositions for integrating the arts into teaching.

As a result, Binney & Smith, Inc. and Northampton Community College entered into a collaborative partnership, *Art as a Way of Learning*®. Binney &

Smith, Inc. committed personnel to the project and provided grant funds for a period of 5 years. Northampton Community College committed early childhood education and visual art faculty and administrators and the use of the Child Care Services early education facility as a demonstration site for the development and dissemination of *Art as a Way of Learning®*.

## Development Phase: Reflecting and Synthesizing

The project divided into a 3-year Development Phase and a 2-year Dissemination Phase. To accomplish the goals of the Development Phase the partnership was immediately expanded to include local school districts and artists. This phase focused on two divergent objectives in response to differing teacher populations: a) a framework for developing an inservice professional development program for early childhood (preschool) and elementary school staff, and b) restructuring the content, format, and pedagogy of the 2-year, associate degree, early childhood teacher preparation program.

Resource teams that reflected the collaborative nature of the project guided the development of *Art as a Way of Learning®* for both the Professional Development Program and the Teacher Education Program. Personnel from Binney & Smith, Inc. and Northampton Community College were members of both teams. The Local Resource Team (LRT) that guided the development of the Professional Development Program also included teachers, art specialists, school administrators, and community artists. The Faculty Resource Team guided the Teacher Education Program.

The Development Phase of both projects involved an intense study of research on the arts, cognition, child development, and excellence in teaching and learning. Team members participated in action research and monthly meetings to discuss the process of collaboration, successes, and struggles with integrated teaching and the benefits to students. The individuals comprising the Local Resource Team and Faculty Resource Team synthesized the body of literature and reflected upon their own teaching to identify understandings which were compatible with and challenging to current teaching practice (Bresler, 1992; 1993).

Research on teaching and learning emphasizes a variety of ways in which children learn and how they come to know and understand the world. These stylistic differences are best met by curriculum rich in opportunities for students to engage in meaningful learning experiences which develop knowledge, skills, dispositions, and feelings (Katz & Chard, 1989). In particular, the work of Gardner (1990) argues that children need multiple ways for expressing and communicating. He states, "Genuine understanding is most likely to emerge, and be apparent to others, if people possess a number of ways of representing knowledge of a concept or skill and can move readily back and forth among these forms of knowing" (Gardner, 1991, p. 13).

Using the context of this information, *Art as a Way of Learning*® developed a Belief Statement, Guiding Principles, and Essential Components which directed the actions of both Resource Teams. The belief states that "the arts, as a language, empower children to construct, communicate, and express understanding and personal meaning" (Pinciotti, Berry, Sterman, & Gorton, 1998, p. 16). This belief and the resulting guiding principles provide the foundation for arts integrated teaching and learning. The five guiding principles are:

1) **The arts are a language**. The arts are symbol systems organized by elements and principles which provide a medium for communicating information, posing and solving artistic problems, and expressing feelings.

2) **Children use art**. The arts are a natural language which must be nurtured and developed so children remain creative and literate in multiple symbol systems.

3) **Art leads learning**. The arts provide a medium for creative and critical thinking.

4) **Teachers guide learning**. The arts provide a central thread to guide and integrate learning across all curricular domains.

5) **Adults are learners and advocates**. The arts, when central to a school, create a dynamic collaborative environment for teaching and learning.

Four essential components, distinct yet interrelated, were evident in highly successful arts integrated teaching and learning. These components included a shared and increased visual literacy, a high level of collaboration, an awareness of the importance of a rich aesthetic learning environment, and use of specific teaching strategies to scaffold and authentically assess children's understanding. Each of the four essential components are woven through the training experiences so that participants have many opportunities to examine, rethink, and construct new ways to teach. The four components, Visual Literacy, Creative Collaboration, Aesthetic Environment, and Teaching Strategies, provide a dynamic, organized format to reflect upon teaching on learning while placing the arts as central to that process.

## Dissemination Phase: Outcomes and Impact

The early childhood teacher education program at Northampton Community College has been restructured so the arts are at the heart of students' learning in the college classroom and in their interactions with children. Unique to the Northampton early childhood program is the belief that preservice teachers must learn to refine and extend their personal artistic literacy and express their own knowledge and feelings in a meaningful way through multiple symbol systems. Outcomes, coursework and assessment are aligned to increase students' understanding, knowledge, and competency in artistic perception, production, and interpretation and to enhance critical and creative thinking skills.

Coursework in early childhood education is infused with aesthetic experiences and opportunities. A new required course entitled, "Art and Visual Thinking," allows preservice teachers to explore and study in-depth the structure, functions, and expressive nature of the visual arts. Each early childhood method course is organized around symbolic modes of expression that relate to traditional early childhood curriculum areas but are approached from their expressive, constructive nature.

Graduates from this program are aware that young children come to school with multiple symbol systems in various stages of acquisition and refinement (Harlan, 1996). As teachers, they are able to plan and implement an arts-integrated environment with explorations based on knowledge of a child's development, culture and learning style. They are cognizant of how symbols are used by children to construct and express ideas and feelings about their physical and social world. But possibly more importantly, as individuals, these teachers use the arts as a system for expressing and interpreting their own ideas and feelings, and as a process for thinking and planning curriculum.

The initial action research and synthesis of ideas by the Local Resource Teams paved the way for *Art As A Way Of Learning: Explorations in Teaching* (Pinciotti, et al., 1998) professional development program. This model program, consistent with the *National Visual Arts Standards* (National Art Education Association, 1994), emphasizes the collaborative and integrated nature of teaching, learning, and assessment, strengthens artistic literacy along with critical and creative thinking, and encourages the design of aesthetic spaces for learning.

Participants in the inservice training collaboratively plan, implement, and refine art integrated explorations in their settings. This begins a process of transforming the arts role from a motivating or supporting activity to an expressive, cognitive process used in learning within and across subjects. Teachers and art educators recognize that children more completely understand concepts and retain knowledge when they use engaging, guided art explorations. These findings are consistent with brain-based and process learning as well as constructivist models of education which shifts the focus of classroom interactions from the teacher and curriculum to children and learning.

Now in the sixth year of the project, over 80 elementary and early childhood schools and 30 community artists have been trained. Implementation of the *Art as a Way of Learning®* model of arts integration can be observed in a variety of combinations from individual teams within a school to entire school projects.

The professional development program expands teachers' attitudes toward art and artistic literacy (Bray & Pinciotti, 1997). Collaborative planning and teaching becomes a vehicle for a shared educational vision and a coherent set of teaching and assessment strategies to guide children's learning. The classroom environment and interactions are more responsive to children's interests and ideas and provide multiple opportunities for joint problem-posing and solving. Children demonstrate what they know and are able to do, as documented through authentic assessment.

Art specialists consistently find their discipline, perspective and creative energy more fully appreciated. They feel more connected to the daily life of schooling and have found new advocates for the arts in their colleagues and parents. This sense of community and regard for the whole child has an expansive impact on the school. Schools look and feel different.

## Lessons Learned And Next Steps

Throughout both phases of the project members of the Resource Teams reflected the creative collaboration model. Even though there was a shared goal and joint commitment each partner, that is, business and education, contributed a diverse perspective, working style, and range of expertise. Perceptions of achieved goals were measured differently between the two cultures. The education partners were satisfied with process and reflection whereas, the corporate culture saw a product as meeting the established goals. Collaboration built respect and was time consuming and energy enhancing with results that often superseded expectations.

Binney & Smith, Inc. and Northampton Community College remain committed to the project as it moves to the next phase. A leadership team, representing business and education, advises and directs the resulting success and new explorations. Grant writing, partnerships with arts organizations, national training sites, and ongoing research are some of the current venues in which *Art as a Way of Learning*® is impacting school reform.

*Art as a Way of Learning*® is a contagious process. Educators, artists, administrators, and business leaders who are empowered to share and collaborate reinvent their development as professionals, while discovering a new level of collegial respect and inspiration. Children who are fully engaged in learning construct meaning through artistic problem-solving, and they ultimately become owners and creators of knowledge. Schools that embrace the arts as a way of learning become exciting educational communities with expanded views on teaching, learning, and artistic expression.

## References

Bray, J., & Pinciotti, P. (1997). Success in education: Creating a community of learners through the arts. *Arts and Learning Research, 13*(1), 79-92.

Bresler, L. (1992). Visual art in primary grades: A portrait and analysis. *Early Childhood Research Quarterly, 7,* 397-414

Bresler, L. (1993). Three orientations of arts in the primary grades: Implications for curriculum reform. *Arts Education Policy Review, 94*(6), 29-34.

Fowler, C. (1996). *Strong arts, strong schools.* New York: Oxford University Press.

Gardner, H. (1990). *Art education and human development.* Los Angeles: The Getty Center for Education in the Arts.

Gardner, H. (1991). *The unschooled mind: How children think and schools should teach.* New York: Basic Books.

Getty Center for Education in the Arts. (1993). *Perspectives on education reform: Arts education as catalyst.* Santa Monica, CA: Author.

Goals 2000 Arts Education Partnership, The. (1995). *The arts and education: Partners in achieving our education goals.* Washington, DC: National Endowment for the Arts.

Harlan, S. L.(1996). *Exploring the early childhood education student's beliefs about art education.* Unpublished doctoral dissertation, Rutgers, the State University, Graduate School of Education, New Brunswick, NJ.

Katz. L., & Chard, S. (1989). *Engaging children's minds: The project approach.* Norwood, NJ: Ablex.

National Art Education Association. (1994). *National Visual Arts Standards.* Reston, VA: Author.

Pearson, B. (1993, Summer). *Inside the arts.* Lehigh Valley, PA: Lehigh Valley Arts Council.

Pinciotti, P., Berry, D., Sterman, C., & Gorton, B. (1998). *Art as a way of learning: Explorations in teaching.* Bethlehem, PA: Northampton Community College.

U.S. Department of Labor. (1991). *What work requires of schools: A SCANS report for America 2000.* Washington, DC: Author.

# Literacy and Visual Culture in Three Art Gallery Settings

Lon Dubinsky

*Canadian Museums Association*

## A Winter's Tale

In 1997 several families, a visual artist, a local historian and staff from the public library and the Dunlop Art Gallery collectively endured one of the worst winters on record in Regina, Saskatchewan. For several weekends between January and March, they made their way around Regina's downtown to develop a self-guided family tour looking at the creatures found in the city's architectural heritage. For the children and parents involved, this was an opportunity- to work on their reading and writing skills, while discovering and documenting some of Regina's architectural history. In the spring, there were additional preparations and in June a tour kit was completed and is now available at Children's Services in the library. It contains a clear and detailed walking tour map, a set of binoculars, a "cheat sheet" booklet for adults on the tour and a take-home guidebook for kids. Families are now able to walk around the downtown core and spot animals, gargoyles, and other mythical creatures on various buildings that are part of Regina's cultural and visual history.

This project, appropriately called "Creatures in Our Midst," was a collaborative effort between the Regina Public Library, long a leader in adult literacy education, and the Dunlop Art Gallery, which is housed in the library and which emphasizes community-based exhibitions and public programs. The project was supported by "Reading The Museum," the program of the Canadian Museums Association to encourage literacy in and through museums that began in 1993. The program, which receives funding from the National Literacy Secretariat of the Government of Canada, has supported 23 demonstration projects thus far and will fund 8 more during 1997-99. Like "Creatures in Our Midst," all are community-based initiatives in which museums work with literacy programs affiliated with libraries, community colleges, social service agencies, and other local organizations. "Creatures In Our Midst" was also one of several projects that involved an art gallery with the aim of extending art education and reaching out to literacy learners beyond the parameters of traditional schooling. What follows is a closer look at "Creatures" and two other "Reading The Museum" projects that took place at the Edmonton Art Gallery in Alberta, in 1995 and at the Art Gallery of Windsor in Ontario, during 1996-97. While approaches to learning through art and learning about art were different for each gallery, all three projects engaged community organizations and confirmed the value of forging partnerships for museum education.

## Museums and Literacy

It is best to first look at the origins of the "Reading The Museum" program and to see how interests in art education, literacy, and community-based learning converged. As Canada's national service organization for museums, the Canadian Museums Association (CMA) continually asks, among other things, who is the museum's audience and is it changing? In 1990, various educational organizations and studies were estimating that over 35% of adult Canadians could not read and write at all or had reading and writing difficulties. The CMA was able to conclude that this large group probably visited museums infrequently or not at all because museums are literate institutions in two fundamental ways. First, since all museums are in one way or another centres of culture, knowledge, and learning, they would appear to be off-limits to people who do not, or believe they do not, possess our society's basic educational credential, i.e. the ability to read and write. Second, if this group were to enter museums they would, in most cases, encounter institutions that rely extensively on text in the form of labels, didactic panels, brochures, and interactive media to explain their contents.

As the CMA considered these implications, it also considered literacy in other ways and in other contexts. For example, how is reading in the traditional sense tied to visual and cultural awareness, both of which are an integral part of a museum experience? How do all visitors, regardless of age or fluency, make sense of the abundant textual material in museums? Perhaps the onus also rested with museum staff, educators, curators, and designers, to use plain and clear language in displays and in complementary textual material. All of these concerns cast further light on the museum's social and educational responsibilities, such as serving specific client groups and working more closely with community organizations.

Using these questions and observations as a starting point, the CMA held a symposium entitled "Literacy and the Museum: Making The Connections." Based on their deliberations, the participants recommended that the CMA undertake several activities to address the particular needs of people who were becoming literate and to examine the textual world of the museum. What emerged was a set of guiding principles that have become the aims of the "Reading The Museum" program, but which also have relevance for museum education generally.

• To make museums more accessible to literacy learners especially adults.

• To promote the use of clear and plain language in museum displays and programs.

- To explore how all visitors make sense of museums.
- To raise awareness of museums as social and community-based institutions.

Faced with this mandate, the CMA had to develop a specific program and this meant examining assumptions and perceptions about literacy, learning, community, and museums. For example, could the CMA expect the museum community to willingly participate in the program? How were literacy organizations and learners to be engaged? What approaches to teaching and learning should be advocated? The CMA also recognized that literacy had come to mean so much more than reading and writing. There was growing interest in visual literacy and scientific literacy, in media, computer and cultural literacy, to cite just a few examples. One thing became clear: the CMA was not about to invent another amalgam and begin promoting "museum literacy." Rather, it recognized from the beginning that museums are places where several literacies are at play, hence the program's aim to encourage literacy in and through museums.

Aware of the great divide between whole language education and the phonics approach to literacy, as well as other instructional methods associated with particular literacy movements, it was decided that the program should not privilege any one approach to teaching and learning. As for projects taking place specifically in art museums and galleries, the CMA program was aware that certain pedagogical methods were favoured and that many of these were inspired by theories of art education. To opt for one particular approach for museum education or literacy learning seemed to run counter to the primary objective, which was to make museums available as an educational resource and cultural source to many groups and individuals. The CMA also recognized that community involvement was a necessary strategy and this meant engaging museum staff, literacy educators, learners, and volunteers with shared or complementary interests. As a result the program began with, and has kept, several components to encourage various kinds of collaboration and partnership. These include demonstration projects, such as the "Creatures In Our Midst" project described earlier. There are workshops for museum staff and literacy educators on clear language and related issues. The program also publishes a newsletter, has a Web page, and distributes learning materials from its projects. However, the program itself does not guarantee effectiveness; local linkages between museums and literacy organizations are critical, thus making the demonstration projects, which are awarded primarily on a competitive basis, the core of the program. Whatever its focus, each project has attempted to meet the needs and interests of learners, both of which Mace (1994) emphasizes are crucial to learning, and especially if adults are the constituency.

One of the signs created by learners in the Art Gallery of Windsor/Multicultural Council of Windsor and Essex County literacy project.

## Learning Through Art and Learning About Art

Within this commitment to diversity and collaboration, several projects have specifically addressed the connections between literacy and visual culture. As noted, with "Creatures," architectural history was the context for developing literacy skills, whereas at the Edmonton Art Gallery, learners put together *Blue Ink in My Pen* (Atkinson, Barreta, Day, Gent, McCaskill, Smuda, Stack, & Woods, 1995), a publication that contained their writing about several works in the gallery. At the Art Gallery of Windsor, students learning English as a second language explored and designed advertising and logos based on their experiences in the gallery and in the shopping mall in which the gallery is located. Looking at "Creatures" more closely, Marzolf (1997), Director of the Dunlop Art Gallery, describes how the project integrated visual and literate components:

> Searching for a way to make stone, masonry and steel animals come to life was a challenge for the learners. Their mission, which they eagerly accepted, was to write a clear, pragmatic and fun guided tour that would bring life to architectural history. This task assisted them in improving various literacy skills, from writing tour instructions that are both practical and entertaining to incorporating information about history, mythology and visual art and participating in decision making with the entire team. (p. 5)

The idea of "incorporating" was the key and it also applied to the project's collaborative aspects, as families worked together to develop the kit with gallery and library staff as well as a local historian and visual artist. Marzolf (1997) also points out that "teamwork" was central from the beginning, as the group initially agreed on four "motivating principles" that guided the project and contributed to its success:

> The group wanted to develop an awareness of visual culture, with the aim of revealing the ideas behind the most banal and overlooked aspects of everyday life and the built environment. The group wanted the tour to be fun. The group wanted people to feel comfortable in the downtown area. The group wanted to create a tour that would encourage atonomous learning, creative problem solving, speculation and questions, including why do architects decorate their buildings with animals? (p. 5)

The comments of learners confirmed how the agreed-upon principles translated into visual observations. Participant Peter Kiraly indicated how the project opened his eyes to architecture. "I never thought of looking at buildings for details, for animals. Our family usually looks for animals in nature, in the countryside" (p. 5). Learner Zora Katic provided another perspective. "Actually, being part of the Creatures project has been a learning pleasure. We could see all aspects of the project—graphics, history, architecture, literature, art and creative writing" (p. 5).

By comparison, the Art Gallery of Windsor took a different approach to connecting writing to visual culture, with its project "Signs and Designs: The Art in Identity." Adults who were learning English as a second language at the Multicultural Council of Windsor and Essex County first studied signage in the shopping mall where the gallery is located. Their observations included keeping a journal of images and words and paying attention to the formal elements of advertising, such as line, shape, colour, form and scale. Inside the gallery, the group looked at several current exhibitions, including one about Clayoquot Sound by photographer Ian Wallace and another about abstraction in Quebec. Goodchild (1997), coordinator of the project, describes the comparisons and contrasts that emerged.

> As this dialogue process grew, the learners moved from a superficial discussion of visual art and advertising to a more in-depth analysis based on their own lives. The conversations led us to action and everyone sifted through reproductions and advertising copy to make a photo-text collage. We also read our work aloud, questioned the art work and discussed what advertisements and visual art could and could not do. (p. 3)

The next stage of the project involved putting theories and observations about design and art into practice, with the production of two signs, one back-lit, the other neon. This entailed working with a neon shop and using a computer graphics program. It also necessitated a discussion of copyright law and artistic property that resulted in the hiring of a model and photographer. Once completed, the signs were exhibited at the gallery, one in a main window that fronts the mall, the other in a hallway/display area of the gallery. The project ended with writing and discussion about the signs produced and about the process that led to their creation.

What is worth noting about this project is its incremental aspects: it began with learners and two organizations, all new to each other and all within the confines of a shopping mall and it gradually incorporated various issues, such as copyright, and several tasks, most significantly the production and display of the signs. While the products and process were different from "Creatures," collaboration was again key to the outcomes which now extend beyond the project. Goodchild (1997) reports that the gallery is developing other visual studies and exercises based on the project, that two of the learners have become active in the gallery's Animateur Program, and that further collaboration with the Windsor Essex Multicultural Council is anticipated.

The Edmonton Art Gallery began on the premises of the Prospects Literacy Association where learners were introduced to what was in store for them at the art gallery. None of the participants had ever set foot in the gallery and felt that they needed some kind of preparation. This initial step was crucial, because during the next 6 weeks at the gallery the students were quite keen to look at works and write and speak about them. Their efforts included recording their individual impressions and producing collaborative pieces in which several students contributed to single stories or poems. The learners also discussed their work, read it aloud and put together *Blue Ink in My Pen*, a catalogue of their writing and the art works. From the initial sessions at Prospects, the gallery became a context for communication that assisted in meeting the needs of students as they practised reading, writing and speaking. It also became more than a medium for learning. Once students realized that they had a rightful place in the gallery, the art works also became sources of interest to them. Lopes, Edmonton's curator of education and project coordinator, explains:

> The students turned the gallery from a place to look at art into a place to create by looking and talking—intertwining visions, thoughts, feelings and meaning, using words as their tools. For five weeks the gallery became a place for envisioning—a creative lab where students tried to puzzle together meanings by writing through them. Paintings, sculptures, installations served as inspiration and were in turn enriched by the developing ideas of those who examined them. (Atkinson et al., 1995, p. 19)

## Curriculum and Place

As the three projects demonstrate, the gallery as a place for collaboration and communication offers great potential for art education and literacy learning that is both practical and transformative. Nevertheless, some educators continue to maintain that the development of skills requires more attention to instruction emphasizing traditional exercises and occurring in conventional sites, such as schools. Other educators welcome art or other forms of education beyond the schools and embrace partnerships, but there is often a tendency to opt for curriculum approaches that serve the schools but may not be appropriate for literacy learners or the gallery environment. For some teachers, the blending of different subject areas and learning objectives inevitably results in favouring certain aims and content at the expense of others. More specifically, some art educators, for example, complain that the arts are often justified and legitimated in term of their usage and applicability for other curricular ends, rather than being accepted for their own value and importance. Burton (1992) puts it this way in a persuasive piece that still resonates:

> It has become fashionable, for example, to argue for the arts in education in terms of their support for other areas of academic learning, such as reading or mathematics. We make claims for the transferability of creativity and critical thinking with almost no solid evidence to back us up. We forget, sometimes, that creativity and critical thinking can be engendered within other subject matter disciplines, when well taught, and that they do not need the arts to enrich them. Such coat-tailing does us little good, for it denies to the arts subjects themselves their own unique and special creative-critical dimensions, dimensions that we are often hard-put to specify clearly, yet which we should acknowledge can not be replicated elsewhere on the school timetable. (p. 13)

I share Burton's (1992) position to some degree when it applies to school curriculum. The arts are usually on the edge of the curriculum and there is a temptation to rationalize and fold them into other areas of learning, especially if they face elimination when schools are forced to make budget cuts. However, Burton's comments can be read very differently if one looks beyond conventional schooling. The projects in Regina, Edmonton, and Windsor suggest what is possible when visual art and literacy converge as opposed to school curriculum focusing on visual literacy or having art in a supporting or subservient role. The projects also demonstrate the possibilities for learning that is community-based in its intent and in its location. In the Edmonton project, for example, the making of meaning developed through a synthesis of visual articulation and writing. As Don Trembath, the writing instructor for the project, points out: "Prospect students came into this project to learn more about art; they leave with a book of their own writing under their arms, and the knowledge that they indeed have something to say" (Atkinson et al. 1995, p. 18).

For the families who participated in "Creatures In Our Midst," combining the visual and the literate in a community setting resulted in some interesting counterpoints, as Marzolf (1997) explains:

> The project also extended the idea of literacy by including visual and verbal aspects, together with an attention to local history and the built environment. For example, the determining factor for including a site was that the creatures needed to be permanent and that the kids, helping their parents develop the tour, had to look for things that would be around

"forever." Try to imagine the literacy exercise in convincing them not to include a "Pheasants Forever" billboard! (p. 5)

For the Art Gallery of Windsor, the engagement by learners with art and advertising worked on several levels:

...there was a clear understanding of what it means to read art and advertising. Questions about how we display our own personal identity and how we understand individual experience were the key questions at the centre of viewing both an exhibition and advertising design. By bringing first-time visitors to the gallery for this project, we brought new eyes to art and we took several steps closer to closing the gap between the two buildings, the art gallery and the mall. (Goodchild, 1997, p. 3)

Suffice it to say these projects suggest that it is advisable to focus less on the place of subjects in a prescribed curriculum. There is great value in concentrating more on the places where learning can happen, provided that the experience is not limited to the "one-shot visits," as Gardner (1991) calls them, that constitute so much of museum education. The importance of place cannot be over emphasized. If much more than lip service is to be given to partnerships, there must be places where individual learners and community groups have a connection and feel some of kind of ownership in where they are and what they do.

## The Future for Community

Much has been written over the last 10 years about how museums must become more responsive and sensitive to the communities in which they are also located and/or whose history they house. This National Art Education Association sponsored collection is evidence of the increasing emphasis on partnerships in art education that go "beyond the school." The three projects described here illustrate the possibilities for collaboration in museum education. There are two obvious but essential factors that contributed to the success of these projects and that evaluations indicate were also at the core of other "Reading The Museum" projects. They also account for why the galleries concerned maintain partnerships with these particular community organizations. First, all participating organizations must have the will to engage in consensus. Enthusiasm can go a long way, but it may not necessarily translate into cooperative action. Second, collaboration takes time and works only if there is trust and mutual respect among the people involved. The projects worked because there was goodwill and consensus, the galleries and the literacy organizations had the trust of their respective communities, and there was a commitment by all concerned to attempt to go beyond the parameters of conventional museum and literacy education.

Partnerships are becoming increasingly prevalent, so much so that they seem more the rule than the exception. The most obvious manifestations are ones driven primarily by fiscal needs, such as corporate-sponsored programs and exhibitions that also attempt to reach out to local and culturally diverse groups. There are also alliances that are making the contents of museums available online and through various multimedia formats. The emphasis on access makes these latter developments appear user-friendly and community-responsive, yet the newest forms of communication and distribution are at best networks for information and exchange. They do not necessarily fulfill local expectations.

Nevertheless, technological realities and challenges strongly indicate what a museum-based literacy program in particular, and community initiatives in general, should now do. There must be attempts to maintain partnerships that meet the needs and interests of people and that occur on site. This is especially crucial for projects that combine visual art and writing, for something is lost if learners do not have the opportunity to make connections between image, text, and place through direct experience.

The "Reading The Museum" program will continue to encourage museums to be more accessible to learners through its projects, workshops, and publications. It must also act further on its initial recognition that museums are "places where several literacies are at play," by addressing the emergence of what a group of educators and researchers called the "New London Group" (1996) identify as "multiliteracies." The group contends that "the multiplicity of communication channels and increasing cultural and linguistic diversity in the world today call for a much broader view of literacy than portrayed by traditional language-based approaches" (p. 60). This is not a new refrain; what is significant is the complexity of the situation and the many avenues of learning, electronic and otherwise, that are now available in private and public life. While the New London Group is concerned with the implications of its position for schooling and pedagogical practice, it also recognizes the educational contribution of community organizations. It may well be that the possibilities for "multiliteracy" in and through museums and related cultural organizations have scarcely begun to emerge. However, what must be constantly kept in mind, as the "Reading The Museum" projects confirm, is the value, if not the necessity, of people-centered partnerships that happen on site in cultural and community spaces and outside traditional institutional settings, such as schools.

## Author Note

I wish to thank Helen Marzolf, Director of the Dunlop Art Gallery, Marie Lopes, Education Curator, Edmonton Art Gallery, and Christine Goodchild, Curator of Education, Art Gallery of Windsor, for their contributions to this chapter. I also wish to acknowledge their dedication to these projects and the enthusiasm and contributions of other museum staff, the literacy educators and, most importantly, the learners. For a complete list and description of demonstration projects and other information about the "Reading The Museum" program, including copies of its newsletter, contact: Canadian Museums Association 280 Metcalfe, Suite 400, Ottawa, Ontario, Canada K2P 1R7 Tel: (613) 567-0099 Fax: (613) 233-5438. The program also has a Web page on the National Adult Literacy Data Base Web site: http://www.nald.ca/rtm/htm.

## References

Atkinson, L., Barreta, P., Day, A., Gent, G., McCaskill, T., Smuda, C., Stack, D., & Woods, L. (1995). *Blue ink in my pen.* Edmonton, Alberta: Edmonton Art Gallery.

Burton, J. M. (1992). Art education and the plight of culture: A status report. *Art Education, 45*(4), 7-18.

Gardner, H. (1991). *The unschooled mind.* New York: Basic Books.

Goodchild, C. (1997). Signs and designs: The art in identity. *Reading The Museum, 3*(1), 3.

Mace, J. (1994). Literacy interests or literacy needs?: Contexts and concepts of adults reading and writing. *Convergence, 27*(1), 58-66.

Marzolf, H. (1997). Creatures in our midst. *Reading The Museum, 3*(1), 5.

The New London Group. (1996). A pedagogy of multiliteracies: designing social futures. *Harvard Educational Review, 66*(1), 60-92.

# The Artemisia Project: School, Artists, University and Museum Partnership

Ann Calvert
*University of Calgary*

Women have traditionally found strength in cooperation, mentorship and group effort. In teaching, artmaking, and increasingly in research, the combined efforts of groups of women have produced remarkable results, and in many cases have meant the difference between idea and accomplishment. The Artemisia Project brought together practicing women artists and high school students with exceptional art abilities to produce a portrayal of the artistic life of those artists within the local community. In the course of the multi-phased project, a number of correspondences occurred: students and their parents met local artists; teachers, researchers, and museum professionals collaborated on the development of teaching programs and resources; school groups were introduced to special features of museum education; and all the participants contributed to the preparation of an ongoing pattern of art resource development.

The Artemisia Project was initiated to improve awareness, access, and opportunities in art for gifted young women students. While it can be argued that these are needs of all young artists-to-be, the difficulties faced by young women in art were my specific concern in this effort. In other writing, I have described the curriculum research and model development, based in theories of gender equity in curriculum, the education of gifted girls, and feminist art theory on which the project was founded (Calvert, 1996). Over a 7-month period, the project integrated the skills and imaginations of 16 high school students, 8 women artists, researchers, teachers, and a museum curator in a term of study, mentorship, artmaking, historical documentation, and curatorship. Local artists and their roles in the community were described and portrayed in a museum exhibition and in a teaching resource package: personal connections between artists and students, and new perceptions about the lives of artists were the most significant outcomes.

The incomplete story of the 17th-century painter Artemisia Gentileschi was the theme for the project. As a woman and assistant to her father, the celebrated Roman painter Orazio Gentileschi, the significance of her artistic contributions to her age went unrecognized, making full documentation impossible for present-day scholars. The Artemisia Project was designed to ensure that knowledge of the lives and work of the eight artists in this study will be conserved.

## Access, Awareness, and Documentation

If young women are to see the positive features of a life in art, they need vivid examples that correspond to their own realities and notions of accomplishment and success. Girls come to art class holding the culturally-ingrained concept that art, as enhancement of surroundings and quality of life, is an appropriate female activity: exploring the content of school art programs and resources (accessible textbooks, art reproductions, slide sets and videotapes), they form the impression that few "serious" artists have been women (Collins & Sandell, 1984; Attenborough, 1996). Powerful myths persist: the true artist is eccentric, solitary, poor, and totally dedicated to work to the exclusion of family, social contacts and material well-being; the art world exists only in Toronto, New York, or Paris. In popular art textbooks and much current art curriculum, artworks and styles are often described by formal and impersonal analytical processes. All of these factors tend to contradict the personal, expressive artistic purposes that draw female students to the subject in their early school years (Huber, 1987; Zimmerman, 1995).

It is difficult for teachers to provide their students with a variety of curriculum resources, biographies, or visual examples of the art produced by women through history. It is even harder, without clear examples, to convince female students that a career dedicated to art can reasonably be combined with other life expectations and lived in their own communities. The need for more complete information is most urgent at the high school level. Students are making decisions about careers and the place of art in their lives. They are concerned about how to achieve a balance between their interests, career aspirations, their expectations for personal relationships, and a way of life that accommodates all of these. Studies have shown that highly capable female art students are particularly needful of realistic information to guide their decisions about careers in various art fields (Foley, 1986; Piirto, 1991). Encouragement is crucial to these potential artists, curators, educators and historians. The Artemisia Project was designed to give future art leaders a close, personal, and local view of real working women artists, and to develop much-needed resources about women in art for other students to explore.

As in the case of Artemisia Gentileschi, many artists whose work is important on the local scene will never be recorded in archives or art historical accounts. Whether or not their achievements ever gain international recognition, they are important examples to offer students of art and art history in their own communities. Erickson and I have argued that students can practice a full range of art historical research skills by analyzing the work and lives of those artists, otherwise undocumented by mainstream art history, who are accessible in their own locales (Erickson, 1983; Calvert, 1993). These arguments are particularly forceful in the cases of women artists whose work often does not fit the mold of art historical analysis, such as textile artists, ceramists, or artists whose work is collaborative, site-specific, and temporal.

## Program Planning: Researchers, Teacher, Curator

The impetus for the project was my ongoing research in art curriculum for gender equity (Calvert, 1996). Naested, an art teacher experienced in programs for gifted students, agreed to host the research project in her school. Ylitalo, the art curator at the Nickle Arts Museum at the University of Calgary, offered her expertise and the Museum's teaching gallery for the exhibition portion of the project. Each of us had specific needs and goals that were to met by the project. The researchers needed access to a group of gifted students. The art teacher and her school needed interesting and challenging opportunities for exceptional art students. The museum needed to expand its audience, demonstrate the educational use of its teaching gallery, and develop a unique, education-oriented exhibition.

The process of planning an integrated project required a great deal of flexibility, delegation, and compromise between partner groups. Some variables were fixed: the teaching gallery of the museum was available for a specific 6 weeks; the duration of the students' involvement in the project was dictated by the semester (the months of September through January), so all their tasks had to be accommodated in that time. Artists had to be found who could be available to the students during school hours. Artists' work schedules, family situations and studio locations were important considerations. Matchmaking between students and their mentors depended as much on weekly schedules, transportation, and distances as it did on mutual interests and artistic aspirations. In working out these details, a fruitful collaboration developed between the organizers of the project—Naested, the art teacher, Ylitalo, the art curator, Latta, a research associate on the project, and me, the researcher.

The various parts of the project, including student research, artist recruitment, mentorship, exhibition development, and resource development were shaped and reshaped by practical considerations, personal interests, and new discoveries. For example, the original purpose of the project was to investigate the effect of a new curriculum model on the attitudes of a homogeneous group of gifted female students, but when the group of interested volunteers included a number of boys, their desire to participate was accommodated. Because grade levels overlapped in the school's art class schedule, participants were of different ages and at different levels in their art studies. We expected to find 8 students to participate in the project: 16 students (14 girls and 2 boys) appeared for the first meeting.

The matching of students and artists was done with deliberate concern for travel times, the artists' work schedules, and the interests and ambitions of the students. The school is in a remote corner of the city, and most of the artists who volunteered to participate in the Artemisia Project lived across town, near the Art College or the University, so travel was a serious obstacle for several students. Many students had after-school jobs, and their other courses caused pressures that precluded leaving the school area for long periods of time. Out of concern for the effectiveness of the project, the researchers were anxious to make the process of visiting the artists as positive and easy as possible. Students were interviewed to gain practical information—who had a car, who had after-school commitments—and more delicate considerations such as shyness and apprehension about meeting the artists, parental approval for travel to a stranger's house or studio, and the student's desire to work with a particular person or art form. At this stage, the teacher was a great help in designating appropriate matches between students and artists. Many problems were solved by pairing students, and once they had made the initial visit, the worries about finding an address and meeting a new person dissolved. Because the project required the students to investigate an artist's life and attitudes, as well as to learn about her working processes, it was important that every student be comfortable about meeting the artist and getting acquainted with her.

## Mentorship: Students and Artists

As students and artists began working together, a variety of partnership styles developed. While each student was responsible for compiling a Portrayal of the artist to which she or he was assigned, personal goals and different circumstances caused each working group to design different experiences, and to find out very different kinds of information about each other. Here are some descriptions of the different partnerships that were formed.

*Evelyn Grant: Humour and Craft.* In addition to interviewing and observing Grant, a ceramist, in her studio, student Michelle Miskey was able to do some of her own work, trying the techniques of casting and assembling earthenware components that mark Ms. Grant's ceramic sculptures. For the Artemisia Exhibition, Michelle completed a ceramic work that adapted one of Grant's themes and her humorous approach. Theirs was the partnership that most closely resembled the artist-apprentice model.

*Jackie Anderson: Design and Function.* Kiima Cato and Aaron Beale, two students with a special interest in clothing design, were paired with Anderson, a jewelry designer. Using precious metals and stones, Ms. Anderson makes wearable forms that can also be displayed on specially designed pedestals, plaques and stands as sculptures. Although the students were unable to work with the expensive materials and processes of jewelry design, several visits with the artist in her studio resulted in the students' appreciation of new concepts of sculpture, jewelry design and the range of forms and objects that are encompassed by the label "art." The students recorded the artist's work in written and photographic forms, and selected examples of her work and their own for the exhibition.

*Marlie Burton-Roche: The Art Teacher as Social Activist.* Tilla Dohler, an exchange student from Germany, and Cassandra Britton learned of Burton-Roche's dedication to the cause of the people of El Salvador through a series of visits to her home studio. Ms. Burton-Roche, a recently-retired art teacher, has gained international recognition as a social activist and an artist, and her painting brings both roles together. Dohler's works incorporated imagery found in photographs Ms. Burton-Roche showed them, and Britton's work, a painting and an essay, described her responses to meeting and knowing Ms. Burton-Roche and her acquaintance with Ms. Dohler. The influences Burton-Roche exerted on these two students were primarily those of theme and purpose rather than technique.

*Mary Lou Riordon-Sello and Joan Caplan: Partners in Process.* This was the largest group, consisting of two collaborative installation artists with five students. Caplan and Riordon-Sello worked together to help their students to appreciate the unfamiliar realms of collaborative and site-specific art, installation forms and processes, and video as art. Rather than visiting the artists' studios, the artists brought their work to the school. At first, the students were skeptical of the value of site-specific and installation art events. The group spent a great deal of time discussing and studying the forms that the artists' work has taken, traveling to sites and galleries, and analyzing how the students' own concepts of art could be related to the work of Caplan and Riordon-Sello. For the gallery presentation, the students and the artists worked together to prepare an installation of images that represented the identities of several individuals. The students also videotaped an interview with the artists that was available for viewing in the gallery during the exhibition. All the works shown by this group were prepared especially for this exhibition, through collaborative planning and consultation. These artists offered the students examples of alternative art forms and purposes.

## Legacy: Documentation and Resources

Each student was responsible for creating a Portrayal of the artist she or he was studying. That entailed studying the artist's working life and artistic achievements, creating a dossier of clippings, catalogues, and interview notes, taking pictures of the artist's work, and selecting and planning the presentation of examples of the artist's work and his or her own work for the culminating museum exhibition. Material from the Portrayals was used in two ways: first, it was presented in the gallery in a study centre as part of the exhibition; second, it was compiled into a package of resource materials for teaching other high school art classes about the artists in the project.

Themes of Identity, Process, and Purpose formed the basic outline of topics and questions supporting the students' inquiry about the artist [see Table 1]. Identity is all the information that can be gathered to portray the character, uniqueness, and place of the artist in the art community in which she lives. Process is all the workings of her artmaking, including the materials and medium she uses, her place and way of working, sources of ideas, and how she presents her work to her audience. Purpose connotes the reasons why she makes art, how her art is received, commissioned, used and understood by others.

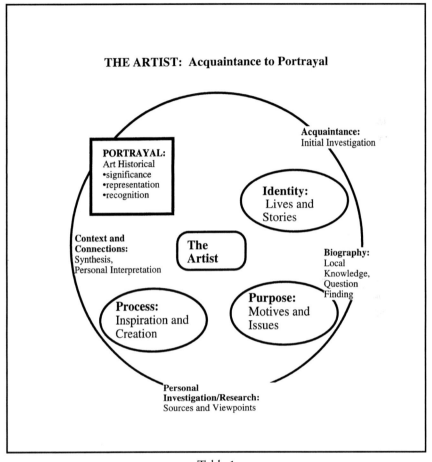

THE ARTIST:  Acquaintance to Portrayal

Acquaintance:
Initial Investigation

PORTRAYAL:
Art Historical
•significance
•representation
•recognition

Identity:
Lives and
Stories

Context and
Connections:
Synthesis,
Personal Interpretation

The
Artist

Biography:
Local
Knowledge,
Question
Finding

Process:
Inspiration and
Creation

Purpose:
Motives and
Issues

Personal
Investigation/Research:
Sources and Viewpoints

Table 1

Within the format, an open-ended procedure was created to encourage the specific character and unique qualities of each situation (student interests, artist's personality, processes, media, environment) to prevail in shaping the Portrayal. The inquiry process encompassed four phases of investigation. Using the study guide, students became familiar with the artist (Acquaintance), described her life and experiences with art (Biography), collected documentary information, recorded her history and analyzed her work (Investigation), and then introduced her and her work to an audience of art students and museum-goers (Portrayal). They were asked to practice investigative techniques, form some exciting questions and then pursue their answers, and finally present a "picture" of their artist-mentor to their classmates and the public through a presentation in class, and then an exhibition at the Nickle Arts Museum. Through these phases, activities enabled them to learn about art criticism, methods of art history, art museum curatorship, and the processes, purposes, and identity of some women artists in Calgary.

## Exhibition: Curator, Students, Researcher

The final phase of the project gave students the challenge of preparing a museum exhibition. Under the guidance of the museum curator, Ylitalo, the student groups selected works by their artists and themselves, planned the placement of the show, and installed the show. She gave them instruction on the processes and requirements of exhibition design. Since the collection of documentary material was an important part of the project, a multi-media study centre was included in the gallery for visitors to read, view and examine their important findings on video and audio, in slides and print files.

For the duration of the exhibition, school art classes and other groups were given tours of the show, and sets of the slides, documents and tapes prepared by the students were circulated to interested schools. The exhibition's accompanying brochure explained the inquiry process and included the question outline, so visitors could pursue some of the same investigative channels that the students used.

As the students pursued their connections with the eight artists, the unique nature of each partnership came into view. Interviews and reviews conducted with the students after the project ended suggested that the students gained a new view of the possibilities of a life in art. They described broader concepts of what art is, where ideas come from, and how artistic interests evolve in their own community. They participated in the making of a legacy of local art knowledge that will serve their fellow students, and they had a chance to exhibit their own work with that of their mentors in a celebration of collaboration and connection.

## References

Attenborough, D. (1996). Feminist interventions in teaching art history. In G. Collins & R. Sandell (Eds.), *Gender issues in art education* (pp. 117-125). Reston, VA: National Art Education Association.

Calvert, A. (1997). Identity and portrayal: Issues of gender in the art curriculum. In R. Irwin & K. Grauer (Eds.), *Readings in Canadian art education* (pp. 91-103). Boucherville, Quebec: Canadian Society for Education through Art.

Calvert, A. E. (1996). An art curriculum model for gender equity. In G. Collins & R. Sandell (Eds.), *Gender issues in art education* (pp. 155-164). Reston, VA: National Art Education Association.

Collins, G., & Sandell, R. (1984). *Women, art and education*. Reston, VA: National Art Education Association.

Erickson, M. (1983). Teaching art history as an inquiry process. *Art Education, 36*(5), 28-31.

Foley, P. (1986). *The dual role experience of artist mothers.* Unpublished doctoral dissertation. Northwestern University, Evanston, IL.

Huber, B. W. (1987). What does feminism have to offer DBAE? Or, so what if Little Red Riding Hood puts aside her crayons to deliver groceries for her mother? *Art Education, 40*(3), 36-41.

Piirto, J. (1991). Why are there so few? (Creative women: Visual artists, mathematicians, musicians). *Roeper Review, 13*(3), 142-147.

Zimmerman, E. (1995). Factors influencing the art education of artistically talented girls. *The Journal of Secondary Gifted Education, 6*(2), 103-112.

# Matrix, Meaning and Meta-Cognition

Cheryl Meszaros
*Vancouver Art Gallery*

Adults leave school, Knowles (1981, p. 57) tells us, knowing how to be taught, not how to learn. Believing that for at least some of its visitors this is true, the Vancouver Art Gallery is developing an approach to learning called *matrix programming*. It is a hybrid of strategies distilled from theories of andragogy (adult learning), postmodern education, current museum and critical theory, as well as from Vancouver's lively street life, and strange and unlikely places such as basketball courts and IKEA stores. The matrix is composed of many fields, nodes and trajectories. Here, just two of its clusters will be explored: meta-cognition and meaning.

The act of learning, the consumption of information, and the production of knowledge, are highly complex operations that are further complicated in the gallery where content and meaning are contested fields. Learning how to learn or *meta-cognition*, involves an epistemological awareness deeper than simply knowing how one scores on a cognitive style inventory, or what is one's typical or preferred pattern of learning. Rather, it means that adults possess a self-conscious awareness of how it is they come to know what they know, an awareness of the reasoning, assumptions, evidence and justifications that underlie the beliefs that something is true (Brookfield, in press). Postmodernism has clearly demonstrated that there is no one, eternal and enduring true interpretation of an artwork, but rather that there are dense clusters of parenthetic meanings that are re-contextualized and recuperated through time. It is the gallery's job to make this accumulation of meaning available to an increasingly wider range of its visitors. Matrix programming is evolving paths, ways, and tools that are making this possible.

The matrix is an amalgamation of processes and products; it exists in the spaces between theory and practice, between the traditional roles of educators and curators, between intuition and imagination, between unmistakable playfulness and rigorous pedagogies, and between the past and the future. Its principles are hybridity, fluidity, complexity, and density. It is mobile and relational, moving so fast through thought that it cannot be apprehended directly, only glanced at askance. It is ephemeral and can only be described through its manifestations.

The program matrix at the Vancouver Art Gallery consists of a number of in-house interpretive sites ranging in complexity from relatively simple informational videos, reading areas and comment corners, to much more elaborate participatory sites such as the Open Studio and dedicated children's activity spaces like the Kids Stops. These will be discussed along with the Animateur talks, and a family program called Supersunday as specific manifestations of the matrix. The Gallery also provides a wide range of recurrent programs including school programs, lectures, symposia, and public forums that constitute another domain within the matrix, which will not be discussed here.

This program matrix is conceived of and examined through a number of different fields: audiences, content, context, cost, educational value, and learning styles. In order to glance at the matrix in an operative form, I will describe the programs designed for the exhibition *Art for a Nation: The Group of Seven*, circulated by the National Gallery of Canada and hosted by the Vancouver Art gallery in the summer of 1996. The matrix is nonlinear, and therefore the order of narration does not imply any order of priority or strict sequentiality.

## Access 1—Kids Stops

Kids Stops are child-centered, hands-on interpretive sites situated in quirky little corner rooms in the main exhibition space. These rooms are part of the legacy of the renovations that transformed the 19th-century courthouse into the Gallery during the 1980s. For many reasons including their awkward location, these rooms where usually left empty. During the Group of Seven exhibition however, they were transformed into bustling activity centers—attracting young and old with their richly colored walls, alluring materials and functional furniture. A printed Kids Stop Guide with a map of the exhibition and instructions led children and parents through each of the stops. The content was arranged as a playful "research trip" through the show focusing on the very distinctive work of Lauren Harris.

The idea of a dedicated children's space in a gallery is certainly not an innovative one. What is new, however, is the multiplicity of roles the Kids Stops played within the interpretive matrix. First, the Kids Stops were spatially dispersed throughout the exhibition rather than being compressed into one space outside the exhibition. Embedding a multiplicity of learning opportunities *into* the exhibition space is an important symbolic statement that learning is valued by the Gallery. Dispersing the sites throughout the gallery ensured a more fluid relationship between the "doing" and the "looking"—where doing becomes one of many ways to access the plethora of meanings surrounding an artwork. The temporal dispersion of the Kids Stops more closely aligned the pace and duration of children's and adults' movements through the exhibition. All of these aspects of the Kids Stops teach both parents and children how to use the resources available in the gallery, and, in some respects, to attend to their own learning processes. Although this is not meta-cognition in its most profound sense, it does open a small space where such learning can begin to happen, and begins to show the potential of the matrix to take on the daunting task of teaching visitors to learn.

Secondly, the activities in the Kids Stops acted as role models for constructing multi-model and methodologically diverse projects within an exhibition: reading, writing, and listening skills were practiced when parents were asked to read sections of the biographical text panels to the children, older children took notes, and younger ones answered questions. Tactile desires were satisfied by a touching station where the differences between raw, stretched, and painted canvas could be experienced. Mirroring impulses were satisfied when children were asked to "sketch" two different Harris paintings that demonstrated his move toward abstraction. Closure was enacted at the last Stop and became part of a rich lesson on symbols and representation when children were asked to make a postcard of their favorite landscape in Canada. Just as certain parts of the Ontario landscape have come to represent Canada as a whole, so their postcard could be a representation of their visit to the show. At each of the Stops there was reading material and sometimes "cheat sheets" for parents who could then feed their children as much information as was appropriate.

Third, the Kids Stops often surreptitiously directed attention to other learning resources. While children walked from Stop to Stop, pausing to do their "assignment" at specific works, they heard fragments of the Animateur's talks expanding on the very themes that they were tackling in their own assignment. This also worked in a reciprocal fashion for, much to our surprise and delight, many adults without children picked up the Kids Stop Guide and used it as a self-guided tour. This kind of connectivity and cross-referencing between different programs is an important aspect of the matrix. It ensures that a deep richness of content is present and available in each of the individual programs, even when those programs are designed primarily for very young children. In a similar light, the sheer multiplicity of roles played by the Kids Stops reflects the density of meanings to which each individual activity is directed. This analogous webbing of form and content is one of the fundamental principles of the matrix.

## Access 2—Animateur Talks

*Animateur* is an upscale name for a paid tour guide. The Vancouver Art Gallery has been experimenting with the duration, format, and content of Animateur talks for the past few years. During the *Group of Seven: Art for a Nation* exhibition, three different Animateurs were stationed in three distinct sections of the exhibition at all times. Each person gave a 15-minute talk at his or her respective station every half hour. The duration of their time was spent answering questions and engaging visitors in conversations. They worked 4-hour shifts and rotated stations every week so as to avoid extreme cases of the "tape recorder" syndrome. The regularity of the tours encouraged visitors to move through the exhibition at their own pace and gave them the freedom to stop, for instance, and watch the whole video if they so chose. Similarly, the between-talk times were long enough so that visitors who chose not to participate in the talks were not forced to do so.

The format of the "station" worked very well for this particular exhibition. The crowds were large enough to justify the density of interpretive staff, and the framework allowed housekeeping to be done at the outset, that is, visitors could be "caught" at the very beginning of the show where the structure of the tours was explained and other interpretive tools identified. Finally, the visitor had the opportunity to experience a variety of approaches, foci, and personalities as each of the Animateurs performed their talks—and perform they did—often to rousing applause.

The content of the Animateur talks and the processes by which they were developed is grounded in principles of density that are integral to the programming matrix. Ideally, the process goes like this. Reading material addressing multiple interpretations of the exhibit's content is circulated to the Animateurs. A series of seminars on interpretive techniques explicate the subject categories and genres of delivery that need to be worked into the Animateur's presentations. The subject categories include contextual, biographical, technical, and anecdotal information as well as references to the theoretical and sometimes contentious issues surrounding the work. Instruction on delivery techniques include communication, voice, and role-playing sessions. Folded into this already dense mixture of form and content is space for each Animateur's individual area of expertise. In the case of the *Group of Seven: Art for a Nation* exhibition, the subject areas were nationalism, feminism, and historiography. Each Animateur then created a series of speaking notes that were workshopped with the team of staff and Animateurs. At this time the conceptual and thematic relationships to other programs were identified and integrated into the talks.

This process of content development welcomes the fine line between communicating the official thesis of a show and creating a space where alternate subject positions can be legitimately voiced within the museum apparatus. At times there is a deeply felt opposition between the two. The strength of matrix programming is that it can embrace, rather than erase, this kind of difference. Traditionally, the power to construct meaning for artworks rested primarily with curators who, trained in art history, prioritized that body of knowledge as the most appropriate way of knowing and coming to understand artworks. The matrix does not marginalize traditional art historical knowledge and methodologies, in fact rarely are the Animateurs without at least one degree in art history. It does, however, hybridize it by adding, multiplying, and creating a space beyond the school, beyond the academy, and beyond hegemony that nurtures the more critical and self-reflective side of meta-cognition. Since debate, contention, and alternative interpretations are available, a greater range of visitors can find the space in which to examine their prior assumptions and beliefs.

The Animateur talk is a very traditional yet enabling pedagogical tool much like reading. In the matrix the content of the talk becomes a model for multiple ways of knowing and coming to know. The power of the matrix is evident in the remarkably deep and poignant conversations that take place between visitors and the Animateurs during the intervals between scheduled talks. Here there are traces and shadows of things that are difficult to discuss because they are essentially internal, unquantifiable, and ineffable. It is in these moments that the matrix is emphatically present and at the same time persistently ephemeral. It is in these moments that current architectonics of learning fail, and it is therefore imperative to find alternatives. The matrix is one such evolving tectonic.

## Access 3—Reading Rooms and Comment Corners

Other ways of knowing and other entry points into the surplus of available meanings are accessible in the Reading Rooms and Comment Corners. The Reading Rooms are rather prosaic, albeit comfortable, places to read exhibition catalogues and to flip through related texts. They are a visually rich and interesting way to provide bibliographic references for visitors. The Comment Corners, on the other hand, are a much more resolute part of the matrix. Physically, they are nothing more than corners of rooms where visitors can leave their comments taped to the wall. Symbolically, though, they are much more. Generally, galleries are more adept at "speaking" (where each exhibition and program is understood as a literal or metaphoric speech act) than they are at listening. Listening tends to take the form of visitor analysis technologies where people's experiences with the works become part of a myriad of statistics, where anonymity and generalizations neutralize the personal and the specific, and where we query only the things that we know how to measure.

The Comment Corner, by visitor analysis standards is unreliable as data because it is not an accurate sample that represents all visitors. Yet within the matrix it is a very important tool for it is one of the few truly discursive sites in the gallery. Textual conversations among and between strangers resides here in the Comment Corners and are a residue of a multitude of different experiences, attitudes and beliefs—the very thing that meta-cognition has us examine. At the same time these conversations are a tiny glimpse into fragments of a democratic public sphere where public opinion, however antithetical to the values and beliefs of the institution they may be, are nonetheless publicly available.

## Access 4—The Open Studio

The Open Studio is a visitor-centered, interactive space designed as a hands-on learning center directly related to one or more exhibitions. It is nestled among the gallery spaces, open during all gallery hours and staffed by full-time Animateurs who welcome visitors, explain the activities and facilitate learning. In its various incarnations over the past 2 years, the Open Studio has housed live bee colonies, plastic cadavers, a walk-in pin-hole camera, a top-of-the line color photocopier, a quilt making project, Polaroid cameras, a mini-art gallery with movable miniature artworks, video tapes of Japanese television, computer stations, and, of course, an abundance of object-making projects from acrylic painting to papermaking and body art.

On a physical level the Open Studio creates a people-centered space within the object-centeredness of the museum by including comfortable, sufficient seating and natural lighting. On a referential or metaphorical level, the Open Studio is coded (i.e, decorated) with references to familiar sites such as the kitchen, living room, patio, the great outdoors, or the quintessential artist's studio. In every respect the Open Studio creates a social space *alongside* the private and sometimes alienating space of the modernist gallery.

Methodologically, the Open Studio, like the Kids Stops, is multi-model and multi-sensory. It is composed of non-threatening activities such as papermaking that do not require what visitors often call talent or skill, as well as more sophisticated "art" activities like drawing, painting, and collage. It is tactile, interactive and diverse, containing music, videos, quiet reading corners, playful fun moments, and serious "teaching" moments. It is intergenerational, children helping parents and grandparents navigate through a computer program, and grandparents showing children how to wield a embroidery needle. Embedded in this diversity is respect for difference including different kinds of prior knowledge, different levels of creativeness and different levels of risk taking.

The Open Studio is densely packed with different ways of accessing information, content and meaning surrounding an exhibition. In some respects, the Open studio is like an UNZIP program on a computer, it is the tool that allows visitors to expand greatly compressed tracts of information, ways of knowing and understanding that they simply could not access by any other node in the matrix, but once accessed reveal immense possibility and profound connectivity.

## Access 5—Supersunday

On the third Sunday of each month the gallery is transformed into a fun-filled learning site for families. The day is called "Supersunday" and includes storytelling, artists' demonstrations, guided tours, up to 10 different hands-on activity stations in the galleries, each monitored by teams of staff and volunteers, a number of studio sites including the Open Studio, as well as interpretive performances relating directly to the exhibitions and including dance, theater, and music, and interesting hybrids thereof. It has been an extraordinarily successful program: between 60-120% increase in attendance; superlative reviews from participants, volunteers and staff; increased financial support both from the gallery and from private patrons; and other galleries beginning to develop programs based on this model.

The model for Supersunday is the matrix, and like a fractal, Supersunday is a micro-version of the matrix. Recognizing that children have radically different ways of accessing and processing information, the learning stations are grounded in the idea of multiplicity. Multiplicity is the key. There are small quiet learning stations and larger noisy ones; there are writing projects, reading projects, storytelling, time-consuming projects, quick projects, standard art materials, and obscure and inventive art materials, and on and on. These are developed keeping in mind Gardner's (1983) multiple intelligences and the Muse project's entry points (Davis, 1996). It is a significant testimony to the strength of matrix programming, that only in retrospect did we discover that the principles of andragogy are also present here in this intergenerational program as well.

The matrix operates in other fields as well. Like the Kids Stop Guide for the *Group of Seven: Art for a Nation* echoed the content of the Animateur's talks, so too the Supersunday activities echoed and are echoed in the school programs, the Intepretive Sites, and other learning stations in the gallery. In our very best moments, the core ideas of the show (contested though they may be sometimes) are present in some way in each of the programs or nodes of the matrix, yet each node is slightly different, as each blade of grass that erupts from a rhizomatic root system is different, each node pointing in the direction of yet another part of the shimmering density of meaning, delight and inspiration manifest at the gallery.

The matrix is located in a space and time that is *beyond schools*. Yet, it is equally *with schools* in a struggle to create places in which learning can take place. For as uncertain though we all may be about the exact course to take or the outcomes of our strategies and realignments, as inattentive as we may have been to what learning actually entails and how it is enacted in our respective institutions, no one can deny that learning is one of the *leitmotifs* of this moment in time. In the very best moments, the matrix points to new possibilities for learning about learning, for making sense of artworks and the worlds they can articulate. It is here where I trust that we will build a future together.

## References

Brookfield, S. (in press). Adult learning: An overview. In A. Tuinjman (Ed.), *International encyclopedia of learning*. Oxford, England: Pergamon Press.

Davis, J. (1996). *The Muse book: Museums uniting with schools in education: A report on the work of project Muse*. Cambridge, MA: Harvard Graduate School of Education.

Gardner, H. (1983). *Frames of mind: The theory of multiple intelligences*. New York: Basic Books.

Knowles, M. (1981). Andragogy. In Z. W. Collins (Ed.), *Museums, adults and the humanities: A guide for education programming* (pp. 49-60). Washington, DC: American Association of Museums.

# Contributors

*Ann Calvert* is an Associate Professor of Art and Art Education in the Faculties of Fine Arts and Education, and Associate Dean (Research and Planning) at the University of Calgary, Alberta. Dr. Calvert's research interests are centred on curriculum theory, gender issues, museum education, and teacher preparation.

*Robin E. Clark* is an Associate Professor of Education and Director of Advisement & Field Placement at Minot State University, in Minot, North Dakota. Dr. Clark serves as Secretary/Treasurer for the Seminar for Research in Art Education, an affiliate of NAEA, while actively pursuing research interests in aspects of artistic motivation, questions of aesthetics, and issues in teacher preparation.

*Robert Dalton* is an Associate Professor in the Department of Arts in Education at the University of Victoria, British Columbia. Dr. Dalton's research interests lie in studio art and multicultural art education.

*Fiona Dean* is an artist and is currently Research Fellow at the Glasgow School of Art, Scotland. Current research interests, supported by the Harold Hyam Wingate Foundation, focus on the changing role of the artist in society and the consequent effects on the relationship between artists, institutions and communities.

*Lon Dubinsky* is a Coordinator of "Reading The Museum," a literacy program of the Canadian Museums Association. He also teaches courses on aesthetics and contemporary art in the Faculty of Fine Arts, Concordia University, and writes, lectures and consults on museum issues, Canadian cultural history and arts and literacy education.

*Rebecca Gorton* is a Professor of Early Childhood Education at Northampton Community College, and coordinator of the *Art as a Way of Learning*® Project. She is active in state and national organizations which develop and advocate for the effective and articulated professional development of teachers.

*Peggy Hunt* is an Associate Professor in the Department of Theatre and Dance, University of Hawaii at Manoa. Dr. Hunt teaches in the areas of youth theatre and dance and creates environmental performances featuring masks, stilt dancing, and giant puppets through out the Pacific Rim.

*Rita L. Irwin* is an Associate Professor in the Department of Curriculum Studies at the University of British Columbia, Vancouver, Canada. While being active in local, provincial, national and international art education organizations, Dr. Irwin also exhibits her own art, publishes widely, and continues her research in the areas of leadership, cross-cultural studies and gender issues in art education using participatory-based methodologies in collaborative ways.

## Contributors (continued)

*Anna M. Kindler* is an Associate Professor in the Department of Curriculum Studies at the University of British Columbia, Vancouver. Her interests focus on artistic and aesthetic development, social cognition of art, multiculturalism, cross-cultural research, and museum education. Dr. Kindler has been involved in a number of collaborative research projects, most recently with colleagues in France and Taiwan, R.O.C.

*Bruno Joyal* is a Professor in the Département des arts plastiques, Université du Québec à Montréal. His main research interests lie in the areas of iconography and ecology. He is very active in local and provincial art education circles.

*Lara Lackey* is an Instructor in the teacher education program at the University of British Columbia, Vancouver. Among other topics, Dr. Lackey's research interests include sociological issues in art and education, adult and non-formal art education, and the inter-relationships among art, education, and leisure.

*Cheryl Meszaros* is Head of Public Programs, Vancouver Art Gallery, British Columbia, Canada. She is the past president of the Canadian Art Gallery Educators, has published widely, taught at several universities in Canada, and has served on a variety of art juries and boards.

*Philip Perry* is the former Coordinator of art education in the Faculty of Education, Monash University, Frankston, Victoria, Australia. Dr. Perry has been an InSEA World Councillor since 1987, and is a Past President, and Honorary Life Member of the Australian Institute of Art Education. He has taught in Australia, Canada, China, England, Russia, and the U.S.A.

*Patricia Pinciotti* is a Professor of Early Childhood and Elementary Education at East Stroudsburg University, and lead trainer for *Art as a Way of Learning*®. Her research interests include artistic development, learning styles, and teacher education.

*Jacques Albert-Wallot* is a Professor in the Département des arts plastiques, Université du Québec à Montréal. His research examines the relationship between the school art style and the world of art. He has been very active in art education in the province of Québec for many years.